MW00954062

Flip the Switch! To a Better you-The Journal
Transform your mindset in just 12 weeks!
Laurina Emiliani ©2023

ISBN: 9798396115668
Imprint: Independently published
Publishing, design, and formatting:
Visions Publishing Group
Miami, Florida

This book is written for you!
If you have a profound inner desire to improve, and
to change your life's direction…
then it is time to do more and be more.

For those people who want more out of life. For those who desire to grow
and reach bigger and better things. For people seeking change, but have no
clue how and where to start, for those who feel stuck and hopeless,
but wish they could make it.

You can make it happen……
If there is a will, there is a way!

All you need is to:

Flip the Switch! to a Better You…

.

This book is dedicated to:

My beloved children, Lucas, and Estefania
Who mean the world to me,
and who are at the centerpiece of my motivation,
my why, and inspiration for everything I do.

Special thanks to:
Michelle and Tiffany Padilla, for your support and encouragement.
To my niece, Lali Mayster for all your amazing ideas.

Special recognition to my dear friends at Corazon Limpio
for all the support provided in the process of healing.
For all we shared and the friendships
that still remain despite of the distance.
To Claudia Estupiñan
for your dedication and tenacity despite immense difficulty.
For the selfless work you do in transforming lives,
including mine.

Special recognition given to John C. Maxwell. The wisdom capsuled in each
one of your books has been of great influence in my life. For all I have
learned, including "The minute with Maxwell" daily messages. Thank you!

Table Of Contents

Congratulations! If you are reading this, it most likely means you have decided to accept the challenge to change the path of your life and embark on the journey of changes this journal will take you through, for the next 12 weeks. The goal is that upon completing this journal your mindset will be transformed as you discover your who, what, where, and most importantly your why.

When I decided to write this journal, I reflected on my life as a woman, mother, parent, and as a business owner. As I started my career and early on, I decided to take the leap of faith and started my own business. I decided to take the challenge of entrepreneurship and it has not been absent of bumpy roads. I made many decisions during the years; some were good, some were not so good, and others were plain bad. As I faced the consequences, those decisions have shaped who I am today.

Along the way I learned many things, one of the biggest lessons I learned is that bumpy roads, and challenging times are the training sessions that help you grow. They are only temporary setbacks that only make you stronger. During this time, despite how bad things appeared be, I always managed to pick myself up and never remained down for too long. I chose to interpret bad decisions and mistakes as lessons, rather than "failures". Some lessons are more costly than others. As such, I learned that everything has an intrinsic value we need to measure within ourselves. I know that despite how bad things appear to be, there is always a solution and a purpose to consider. Fulfilling "our calling" is a key element we can't set aside in our lives.

This journal reflects on the path of growth I have experienced for myself as I have confronted the reality of having lack of motivation after 25 years in business. After all these years, and a successful career, why was motivation absent at this point in my life? I decided to discover why I was not motivated to continue and had a deep desire to search for what I am passionate about. One thing was clear to me, ...what I was doing was not something I desired to do for the rest of my life, and I was not about to continue to live unfulfilled. I was ready for change!

As a result, God took me down a different path, and in that path, I have discovered my true "Why", my true passion and purpose in life. I discovered my passion to give, to add-on value, and to edify people who lack direction and feel lost and frustrated feeling unfulfilled and living un-purposedly. I've been there, I've done that, and now I can share my life experiences. I spent a good portion of my life feeling frustrated, lost, and trapped in a career that while it has been handsomely profitable, it was no longer fulfilling. I felt there was something more profound to give, something more significant to accomplish. Through this journey I learned one important lesson. When you follow your passion, you don't work, instead you perform. Whatever it is you do, you give it all you got, you enjoy it and do it with love.

One day I said to myself, maybe I should share with others the steps into how my eyes were open, and my heart affirmed by discovering the Who, the What, the Where, and the Why in my life.

This journal will help you envision yourself short-term and long term. It will be a planning tool to set and accomplish goals. It will help you stay organized, and it will be your "SAP", the Secret Accountability Partner we all need.

Thank you for opening the door of opportunity. Thank you for allowing me to plant the seed of growth in your life. Flip the Switch! to a Better You Journal will take you step by step to becoming the ideal you. Be ready to re-discover yourself and to implement the changes you need today, and to live a purposely fulfilled life moving forward. It doesn't matter where you are today, what matters is where and who you will be tomorrow.

Be ready to *Flip the Switch! to a Better You...*

My decisions in the past shaped who I am Today.

The decisions I make today,

will shape who I will become tomorrow.

The

Journal

Flip the Switch!
...To a Better You

Transform your mindset in 12 weeks!

And

Align with your purpose to reach success.

Week One: Transparency

Day One	Date:
	No change, No Breakthroughs

Where are You?

The first two things we look at when planning a trip are: 1) where will I depart from, and 2) my point of destination. This is because determining the point of departure and destination will help you plan the trip with more ease and precision. Same applies to our lives and the business or career you plan on launching sometime down the line in our lives.

To take full advantage of this journal, you need conviction and full commitment to change, and to implement those changes. Upon completing the tasks, you will see transforming results. Remember, to see results you must be prepared to be brutally honest with yourself. Allow this to be between you, and God; you, and your creator, or you, and yourself, depending on your beliefs. If you want to discover and fulfill your purpose, you must be honest and truthful throughout this journey.

Diagnosing is always the first step to healing. A doctor will never be able to look for a cure or treat a disease without proper diagnosis. So, the first step in this journey will be diagnosing where you are right now. You may not like what you are about to uncover but be assured the rewards will outweigh any discomfort. Allow discomfort to be part of the process. Come to terms with the fact that there is no growth in your comfort zone. As you experience discomfort, and you step out of the comfort zone, you know you will encounter growth down the path to your destination. Growth will join the ride and it will be a very pleasant experience. Don't be afraid to step outside your comfort zone. You may experience fear and even some pain, so let fear speak to you. It always carries a message. It is part of the growth process. Remember, "No pain, No gain".

Let's start your trip through this journal for the next few weeks by going through the diagnostic process. Remember to be honest and truthful. You overcome when you confront. To heal pain, you must confront the pain. To heal from fears, you must confront fear. Don't hide or run away from it, rather confront whatever is keeping you bound, recognize it, but don't surrender to what's holding you back. Then, once you confront, you can heal and move on.

Things to Ponder

1. Where do you stand right now, personally, and professionally?
2. Do you feel stuck or disoriented? Or do you feel you have some traction in life? Elaborate…

Notes:

_____

_____

_____

_____

_____

_____

_____

_____

_____

_____

_____

_____

_____

_____

_____

Week One: Transparency

Day Two   Date:

To grow requires transparency!

Who are You?

K nowing oneself may not be an easy task. Our life is a compilation of experiences and situations. The way we internalize events, situations, and the way we think, in other words our mentality is what shapes who we are.

The best way to start this process is by practicing introspection. Pay attention to yourself, what you think, the way you think, how you speak to yourself and others, and finally, how you respond and react to situations. Be conscious of your emotions, and the feelings these emotions trigger. Examine yourself, identify any feelings causing pain, and where they stem from. Pain can transform a life, for better or for worse. You need to be aware of how situations affect your emotions and how do they make you feel. Because of your emotional state, you may be more vulnerable to feeling intimidated, or maybe manipulated by people around you. Are you paralyzed by fear? Perhaps you feel insecure? Pain manifests itself through your emotions. but no matter how pain manifests itself, don't be afraid to confront it. Cry if you must as you get intimate with yourself and uncover certain truths you may otherwise would have never faced. It is all within the process.

As you confront pain, as part of the healing process, you need to forgive, forgive others, and forgive yourself for putting up with whatever situation you have lived or currently living through. As you forgive, crying may very well be what you need to let go of the past. Identify the chains that are holding you in bondage. Perhaps addictions to people, substance, food, behaviors, or comfort zones. Get in touch with the real intimate you, not the person you pretend to be to please others.

Take off the masks! Take your time, this may be something you need to think about somewhat profoundly. The clue is getting in touch with your intimate self, your emotions, feelings, your fears, your dreams, your wants, and needs. Examine the things you dislike about yourself and ask yourself why you dislike them so much. Get ready to meet the real you and take steps to transform into the best version of yourself.

Things to Ponder:

1. Are you true to yourself? Are you genuine to your yourself, to family, friends, co-workers and/or customers?
2. When, where, and how are you that person who you are not, but is, as you seek to belong or seeking attention? Do you wear masks?
3. Who are you? Who is the real you...without masks?!

Notes:

_____

_____

_____

_____

_____

_____

_____

_____

_____

_____

_____

_____

_____

_____

_____

_____

_____

Week One: Transparency

Your Personality

According to the DISC method, there are four basic personality types. Although we can be a combination of the four, we all have one dominant style. The best way to determine with accuracy is to take the assessment test.

These are the four DISC personality styles:

D

DOMINANCE:

They are bold and skeptical, and they place priority on "Winning". They pursue challenges and can be easily irritated with opposing points of view. They are often perceived as indifferent and somewhat hostile. However, they are out-going enthusiastic and optimistic people who are fun to be around. They are *task oriented* multi-taskers, with a strong determination towards their goals. Because they are more results-driven, money may be their center point of motivation.

I

INFLUENCE:

They can be both bold and accepting *people-oriented* individuals who enjoy making connections. They tend to be welcomers who ignite excitement with their enthusiasm and high energy. However, they lack attention to detail and fail to follow-through. Their relationships may not be long-lasting. They are optimistic, bubbly and highly expressive. They are good to have around when things go wrong because they are great motivators and excellent encouragers. They are motivated with attention, awards, and public recognition.

S STEADINESS:

This is a *people-oriented* style who is accepting but may appear to be somewhat cautious at first glance. They are highly motivated by helping others, adding value, and master the art of giving. They are calm, tolerant, and patient. They are thoughtful and respond to challenges in a very methodical problem-solving style. Empathy is a strong trait as they enjoy providing support. They struggle with change, but once their temporary daze clears, they are highly motivated to achieve effective results.

C CAUTIOUS:

They are *task and detailed-oriented* perfectionists who work best on a stable environment. They are very collaborative and enjoy sharing their expertise to improve the quality of work and work environment. Change is not their strongest trait, as they are driven by logic, and have the tendency to overanalyze things with a good measure of skepticism. They are a good source of objective support and objective view of situations.

(Take your DISC Assessment test by visiting www.laurinaemiliani.com and scheduling a coaching session).

Things to Ponder:

1. How do you see yourself in this chart?

_____

2. How would you describe yourself?

Notes:

_____

_____

_____

_____

_____

_____

_____

_____

_____

_____

_____

_____

_____

_____

_____

_____

_____

_____

_____

_____

_____

_____

_____

Week One: Transparency

Day Four   *Date:*

The perception I have of my environment becomes my reality.

Self-Perception

Experts state that in early childhood, around the time we enter preschool, we start becoming aware of our environment and of ourselves. This awareness will give you or take away the ability to grow and become whomever you decide to be. Unfortunately, not all your life's experiences are positive and edifying. Your life is built from a flow of events all the way to adulthood. You are shaped by this flow of events; your mindset is programed by the interactions you have with others and as a result, these interactions play a critical role in the way you perceive life, others and yourself.

You have the power to create or to destroy with things you say and the things you do. Sometimes this power to create is snatched from your hands by the belief systems adopted along your life. This belief system acquired along the line, will ultimately determine who you become.

We all have an inner critic. The trick is not letting the inner critic take over your thought process and allow it to entangle you in an inescapable set of failures. It is all tied to your belief system and the perception you have of yourself. Your awareness will lead you to the top or will keep you frustrated at the bottom of the pit of misery. Who you believe you are will reflect on your accomplishments and how other people perceive you. This will label you for better or for worse.

This journal will help you raise your awareness to replace any negative perceptions you have of yourself with a positive perception helping you create a better future and a better life for yourself.

Things to Ponder:

1. If you had to describe yourself, how exactly would you do so?
2. What is your opinion of yourself?
3. Describe the ideal you?
Notes:

_____

_____

_____

_____

_____

_____

_____

_____

_____

_____

_____

_____

_____

_____

_____

_____

_____

_____

_____

_____

_____

Week One: Transparency

Day Five   Date:

Trust is earned, let your yes be Yes and your no be No.

Trust

When a person is said to be trustworthy it means that their actions meet their words. In essence, "say what you mean and mean what you say". You need to establish how valuable the No's and the Yes' are to you and to people around you. When trust is present, it is easier to engage in relationships, in a project, in a conversation, or whatever is going on around you. Trust is earned, not voluntarily given. Thus, to earn trust, you must be willing to contribute, to give, to share your dedication, provide input, your thoughts, your positive vibes, and your energy. You can feel the positive energy flowing in healthy relationships, but when trust is lost the opposite is true. When bad vibes invade a relationship, a project, or your environment, you will experience total breakdown. It is difficult to mend relationships whenever trust is breached. Trust takes time to build, great effort to earn and can be completely lost with just one action or just a few words.

The goal is to be or become a trustworthy person. You want to be able to *earn* trust. It is a personal choice you make, a commitment to follow through your personal choices. Your yes must be a firm yes, and your no must be an unequivocal no. You can't waver between the yes and the no. The consistency of your actions with what you say will make you worthy of trust.

Things to Ponder:

1. Am I worthy of trust? Is my yes, a "Yes" and my no, a "No"?
2. Do I waver to my commitments?
3. Are you on time to your engagements? Is there consistency between your words and actions? Are you dependable? Can people depend on you fulfilling commitments?

4. Why? Elaborate on this thought.

Notes:

_____

_____

_____

_____

_____

_____

_____

_____

_____

_____

_____

_____

_____

_____

_____

_____

_____

_____

_____

_____

_____

_____

_____

_____

Week One: Transparency

Day Six   *Date:*

What you see when you look at yourself in the mirror,

Will determine how others see you.

Self-Esteem

We have no guarantees in life, no one does. But there are people who despite circumstances, inherently good or bad, can overcome and recover from life blows succeeding at whatever they decide to do while others spend their lives on the hamster wheel, never moving forward despite their efforts.

What is the difference between a person who succeeds and a person who doesn't? This is mainly determined by perception and mindset. Your deeds are like seeds in life. The things you say and do are seeds you sow. What you think you can do will determine how much land you make available to sow the seeds. If you have a limiting mentality the amount of land available for you to plant your seeds will be small; therefore, the harvest will be limited thus, lacking abundance. But if you have a positive stance in life, the amount of land available to you will expand, opening for more opportunities to grow, and the harvest will inevitably be far greater and abundant.

The opinion of yourself reflects on how you see yourself against life adversities and challenges. The judgment calls you make upon yourself is a clear determining factor of your self-esteem. Today you need to consider the opinion you have of yourself and the how you project yourself to others. For change to be effective you need an accurate diagnosis. Think of this journal as a scanning device helping you look deeper inside yourself for better transparency. This is the time to diagnose your self-esteem and your self-perception and to do so, these are a few things you will need to consider.

Things to Ponder:

1. How do you see yourself when faced with challenges and adversities?
2. Do you feel you are confident, and can you recognize insecurities?
3. Do you have limiting thoughts? Or do you thrive with a winning mentality?
Notes:

_____

_____

_____

_____

_____

_____

_____

_____

_____

_____

_____

_____

_____

_____

_____

_____

_____

_____

_____

_____

_____

_____

_____

_____

Week One: Transparency

Day Seven   *Date*

Self-reflection may be uncomfortable, but necessary for growth.

Day of Reflection

One advantage to having time of reflection is gaining self-awareness. If you don't take time to look at yourself and reflect on who you are, you may be living life playing the wrong role in your Broadway show. To optimize your life, it is important to take a good look at yourself and know who you really are.

Take some time today to see your reflection on the mirror, be honest and determine who you are. Make an effort to capitalize on the attributes you like of yourself as you make the changes you need to move forward into the right direction in the path of growth and success you desire. Set aside time for reflection, it will help you discover, learn, and grow.

Reflect on what you have learned this week about yourself, and your life.

Things to Ponder

1. Using what you have learned so far about yourself, can you recognize something or somethings you would like changed or improved in yourself and in your life?

Notes:

_____

_____

_____

_____

_____

_____

Day One   Date:

When we seek growth, we must endure pain.

Dealing with Pain

Pain is inevitable, in life you will experience tribulation, trouble, disappointment, loss and many other negative experiences triggering emotions that will, without doubt, dent your heart. If we all have bad experiences, and we all do…why are there some people who can deal with problems successfully and others who don't?

On the one hand you have people who brush things off with ease, overcoming obstacles without internalizing events. As a result, they will not allow negative events and emotions affect them. On the other hand, have more difficulty dealing with life's challenges unable to bear with situations. They become targets, vulnerable to the indiscriminate darts thrown at them. In our everyday life, there are many darts of all sorts aimed at us.

Often, these people don't do well confronting pain and look for ways to numb or run away from pain as their way of dealing with it. As a result, they fall prey to different addictions to escape from the negative feelings they can't confront. They are not emotionally strong to deal with pain. As you grow you become stronger. This journal will give you the tools to help you discover how to confront and deal with pain in a positive way. The fact is that we all have a "pain drawer", some drawers are bigger and with more stuff stored in them than others. It's time for some spring cleaning!

Pain can be physical. Physical pain may be a sign of a weakness being conquered, such as the pain and soreness when working out. Your muscles are weak and through workout they become stronger. Pain is a sign the body emits to communicate. Pain may also be a sign of sickness, your body signaling something is wrong. Whatever it is, pain can't be ignored. It must be confronted and pursued for healing. You must know that while pain is a negative experience, it is a red flag carrying an important message that may guide to healing when not ignored. Dealing with pain leads you to diagnosis taking you closer to healing and therefore freedom.

Emotional pain has its own symptoms, giving signs of a more serious underlying problem. If you don't look for the root cause, wounds and pain will haunt you forever. Emotional pain is caused by wounds from events in our lives. It can be as simple as experiencing bullying, a condemning phrase by a teacher or a demanding parent. It can also be caused by the shocking loss of a loved one or by having experienced some type of abuse. No matter the source, you must confront pain and find a way to heal the wounds to eradicate its consequences.

If you are looking for personal growth you must confront pain no matter how it's manifested. You can look for counselors, psychologists, doctors, and coaches to help you resolve the issue but unless you search within yourself, no help will ever be enough. Don't be afraid to deal with pain, the rewards are far greater than enduring pain, no matter how comfortable you feel.

Take some time to dig into your heart and uncover the hidden feelings. Get out of your comfort zone into the healing zone! Keep in mind that you must remain honest with yourself and with others. This is about discovering the source of pain and dealing with it. If you want to be free, you must clean house, uncover all the rot and treat it. Otherwise, the rot will continue to expand, and the longer it remains untreated, the worse it will get.

Things to Ponder:

1. What's in your infamous pain drawer? …We all have one!
2. What wounds have you filed away in the "pain drawer" that you have been struggling with? What pain file are you ready to deal with today?
3. Are you afraid to uncover the pain? How afraid are you? What emotions does it trigger?

Notes:

_____

_____

_____

_____

_____

_____

_____

_____

_____

_____

_____

_____

_____

_____

_____

_____

_____

_____

_____

_____

_____

_____

_____

_____

_____

_____

Week Two: Pain

Day Two   Date:

Offenses are like sharp arrows,
they will not cause harm unless they hit a target.

Feeling Offended

As we reflect on pain, we can't ignore offenses. Often, pain originates with words or actions, some are ill intended, some are not. Ultimately, offenses have no effect unless they have a place to land. Understand that you must accept the offense for it to cause you harm, otherwise it will not fulfill its purpose. If you don't receive it, it won't hurt you! You can't receive everything handed to you. Think of offenses as a plane, your heart as the runway and your mind as the control tower. A plane may be circling above the runway asking for permission to land, but until the control tower gives it the green light the plane will be unable to land. Therefore, next time just refuse to give offenses permission to land. Offenses may be ill intended, but they will not hurt you if you refuse permission to land.

You must be in the right mindset to refuse ill intended words and actions to land in your heart. Your mind and heart must be prepared, like a soldier prepares for battle. You must also prepare yourself to confront and fight off all these offenses aimed to hurt you and this my friend, is inevitable.

Be conscious not to allow words and actions to wound and harm your heart. You can't spend your life in an emotional emergency room. You must take charge and get your mind in shape to fight off these ill intended darts often aimed to hurt you. Understand not everyone has your best interest at heart. I am not implying to live a defensive untrusting life. I am saying you must guard your heart because your life flows from it, literally. Think about this, what authority do people have over your life that their opinion would be so meaningful to allow their words to wound your heart to the point of extreme disappointment? The answer to that question is, the authority you and only you decide to give them.

You also must also take things depending on who they come from. There are a lot of people with sick hearts. You can't allow your heart to be contaminated with their sickness. All the bitterness, envy, ill intentions that stem from a sick heart will entangle you if allowed.

In addition, if you are easily offended it is often evidence of pride and lack of humility. Not accepting truth, being closed minded to constructive criticism, and acting as if you are all-righteous and never wrong is also very negative. If so, pride is to be handled and worked on without delay. There must be a balance!

These are two important points to consider:
a) You must be open-minded, and humble enough to accept when you are wrong, and b) You must also be cautious of who is giving you advice and opinions.

Pride is the entrance hall to failure, and that is a door you may not want to open. However, if its ever opened make sure to correct and learn. Pride is the inability to admit when we have failed, or when we miss the mark. Pride will look for excuses unable to take responsibility, blaming others and that will only lead to stagnation. Pride will never lead to growth.

A prideful heart will be easily offended because it lives and feeds on entitlement rather than gratefulness. It will always lead to failure and failed relationships. We are relational beings, thus when in failed relationships, we will seldomly feel the sense of belonging we all crave within our circle. If you diagnose pride in your heart, it's time to serve it with an eviction notice. Boot it out!

Stay humble! Humbleness is a virtue that is often misinterpreted as weakness. To the contrary, humbleness is a virtuous attribute in the ability to admit when we are wrong. This enables you to take corrective actions necessary to move forward in the right direction to succeed.

Things to Ponder:

1. Do you get offended easily? If so, could it be pride, low self-esteem, or your internal insecurities?

Learn to refuse offenses, don't receive everything you are handed. Remember you are the control tower, and you can refuse to open the runway. Try to dismiss offensive remarks. Remember the adage: "Silly words, deaf ears".

Notes:

_____

_____

_____

_____

_____

_____

_____

_____

_____

_____

_____

_____

_____

_____

_____

_____

_____

_____

Week Two: Pain

Day Three   Date

You can never reach success without the bitter taste of failure and bad

decisions.

They are the lessons that lead to growth.

The Pain of Failure and Bad Decisions

We have been taught to believe failure is a negative experience. To fail is to lose and losing is just falling short of the mark. Failure has such a negative connotation that the mere thought of failing prevents some people from trying. Making bad decisions and experiencing failure is part of the growth process, gaining experience, and therefore reaching a higher level.

Michael Jordan, renown NBA player of the mid 80's and 90's and recognized as one of the best of all times, has a very interesting story. Michael was not chosen for the Varsity team when he was in his sophomore year of Highschool. Michael was simply not selected for the Varsity Highschool basketball team for a good reason, he wasn't ready! He was a skinny 5'9" sophomore player who aspired a university selection, but he did not have much to offer to the varsity team at the time. Michael Jordan needed time to develop as a player, and he was given an opportunity to do just that in the Junior varsity team. He did not fail when he was held back. He was being formed! He may have interpreted the experience as a failure and allow his career to be demolished by this holdback. Instead, he persisted in building himself as a basketball player. At the time, he experienced the pain of inexperience and for a moment he may have felt he had failed. Michael developed his skills; he grew physically and mentally as he continued his training to stardom. His coach made the right decision by not choosing him too early. The path of his career shows he was at the right place, at the right time.

One of the biggest strengths of Michael Jordan was his mindset. The fact that he was held behind made him mentally stronger. Thus, our mindset, the way we process information and events in life is a strong determinant of outcome. That sets winners apart from losers, winners never give up and losers throw the towel when facing disappointment. Losers are not strong enough to handle challenge and overcome adversity. Winners are challenged by adversity.

One thing is basically guaranteed, we will make mistakes, bad decisions, and fail at things we try at some given point in our lives, despite the level of knowledge and experience we may have. One missed judgment call can lead to loss and/or failure. Knowledge and experience are no guarantee against failure. The best antidote to failure is our mindset, our mentality, how we process challenges, failure, and disappointment. At the end of the day, it's not how many times we fall, rather how we recover from the fall that counts. Don't play victim, don't expect anyone to come to your rescue. Instead, take responsibility, pick yourself up and go!

Throughout this journal you will have the opportunity to challenge yourself to make the necessary changes to transform your mindset. After twelve weeks you should have the information to make the changes to improve the way you think and the way you process information. Therefore, your chances at succeeding against challenges will greatly improve by implementing changes setting yourself apart from those who fail.

Tell yourself: "I am a winner, and I will overcome!" Learn to feed your mind with the right messages. Make sure they are positive, motivating, and inspirational.

Things to Ponder:

1. How do you handle challenges or disappointments?
2. Do you break, or do you get motivated?
3. How do you interpret setbacks, as challenges or roadblocks?

Notes:

_____

_____

_____

_____

_____

_____

_____

_____

_____

_____

_____

_____

_____

_____

_____

_____

_____

_____

_____

_____

_____

_____

_____

_____

_____

_____

Week Two: Pain

> *Day Four*   *Date:*
>
> *Happiness is not the lack of disappointment,*
>
> *it's a decision despite of circumstances.*

The pain of Conflict and Broken Relationships

Some of us can handle conflict very well, some others much rather avoid conflict at all costs. Despite of how we handle conflict, it is a disrupter that messes things up for a lot of people.

Loss is at another level of pain and it's a complicated process for our hearts to handle.

Loss is always painful, having to let go is never an easy task. It's the release, the disconnection, the detachment process that makes letting go so difficult. Bear in mind we will all experience loss at one given point in life. The loss of a loved one, or a broken relationship are two of the most painful experiences anyone will face in their lifetime. We can also experience financial loss, which can also inflict pain and may be difficult to cope with as well. Giving up the fruit of years of effort or losing a job which means the income security for a family can be devastating. No matter the type of loss, we all deal with loss differently and we must learn how to cope, learn to release, and let go. It is particularly important to process the information of loss in a way that will allow for growth and not stagnation. We can choose to learn and turn the page, or we can dwell on the loss and fester.

If we choose to learn and move on, we have greater chances to overcome the challenge. But if we remain dwelling on the loss we will linger in a place of emotional decay with negative ramifications. Pain can lead to anger, bitterness, and depression, to name a few, keeping us from moving forward. Having the right attitude will allow us to leave the pain, suffering and loss behind and be ready to continue our journey.

When dealing with loss, it's necessary to mourn. Grief and mourning are part of the healing process, but we can't mourn forever. Mourning has its time under the sun. You must move past the mourning phase and act upon what comes next. Please realize there is not one thing you can do about the loss itself. You can accept your reality and work to use it for better and not for worse. To do this you must remain positive despite of circumstances. At one point you need to move past the mourning phase, otherwise you will fall in a pit of self-pity where nobody can pull you out, but yourself.

Remaining positive and adopting a positive stance before negative circumstances is a muscle we must work out and grow strong. The more we practice it, the better we become at it and the stronger we become. We need to train our brain to remain positive. To recover we must not dwell in the pain and intentionally continue to push forward as soon as possible. It's the only way we will shift to a positive outcome despite of circumstances. Circumstances should not dictate the outcome in your life! It's about time you claim your life and own it.

Things to Ponder:

1. What loss or broken relationships have you experienced?
2. Is there pain in your heart that is holding you back?

Notes:

_____

_____

_____

_____

_____

_____

_____

_____

_____

_____

Week Two: Pain

Day Five   Date:

Pain triggers courage, Courage triggers action

How to Use Pain to Grow

Pain, loss, and failure are words that make our hearts cringe. It's not something we welcome, but necessary to learn and grow. We can't fully develop without experiencing disappointment and overcoming pain at any given point in our lives. It is just part of life. Failure, loss, setbacks, and pain will teach us lessons we wouldn't learn in a classroom. It is a prerequisite for growth and development.

I first heard the expression "hugging the cactus" at "Corazón Limpio" or "Clean Hearts", a ministry in Davie, Florida dedicated to providing inner healing to those who seek for help. This ministry helps people deal with behavioral issues through a program to overcome behavioral addictions. Hugging the cactus is a term often used by recovering addicts to describe the point when people tend to hold on to the pain, and the cause of pain because it is what's familiar. When we hug the cactus, it should remind us of what is causing the pain to overcome denial. Denial is part of the initial stage of the healing process. It's important not to remain in our comfort zone despite the pain. The cactus identifies the pain; thus, we should not hang on to the cactus too long. In other words, don't hang on to the pain, as if it was dear life.

Addicts for example, hug the cactus when they turn back to their addiction refusing to let go of what is causing them pain. Addicts, need to break the habit and the habit is the cause or the root of pain. Many, refuse change because change takes effort and mainly what keeps them bound is the fear of what change will bring. Some others, rather stay where they are because of the fear of failure, they think failure is inevitable therefore it's not even worth trying. What needs to be clear is that when we quit trying, we basically sign a guarantee for failure. Not trying is not failure, it is way worse. Giving up is yielding your better self, your dreams, and goals to a hopeless state of futile stagnation.

To heal, you must deal with the root of pain. If the tree is ill, the fruit will not taste good. It will be stale with no flavor, or it will have a bitter/sour taste rather than sweet and tasteful. Therefore, to heal the tree means to treat the root. Once you deal with wounds at the root level, and the root is healed then you are empowered to move forward. Otherwise, you will remain hugging the cactus, looking to numb the pain with external forces that won't address the pain, rather ignore it. You must address the source of the pain to heal and move on from the place of discomfort to a place of relief. In other words, from your comfort zone to your productive zone. The first step to healing is to stop denying the facts, and accept the reality of loss, failure, or disappointment. Accepting the facts means you accept the need for "change". Once your heart accepts it and you are settled with that reality, then you can move on; but until then, you are stuck in the pit of self-pity and misery unable to gain ground in the growth process. To sum it up, "Stop Hugging the Cactus"! Are you ready to confront the pain? It's the only way to freedom!

Things to Ponder:

1. What can you identify as your cactus? The pain and the root cause of the pain.
2. Are you hanging on to the pain or are you willing to set yourself free?

Notes:

_____

_____

_____

_____

_____

_____

_____

_____

Week Two: Pain

Day Six   *Date:*

After a storm, there is always a bright sunny day!

Grief is Necessary for Healing.

Grieving is a necessary step through the healing process. When we face loss, we first tend to fall into denial as we refuse to admit the truth and the reality of circumstances. We hug the cactus to remind ourselves we need to admit we are hurting, to surrender ourselves and to let go. Once we are brave enough to admit it, we then move into the *anger* phase characterized by asking ourselves "why" instead of "what for". Persisting on answering the "why" question will inevitably lead you to falling for a victim mentality thinking everything happens "to you", thus falling prey to this negative state of mind. This is one of the most difficult states to snap out of as it becomes a down spiral fall keeping people trapped in a negative mindset. Bad things do happen to good people, it is a reality we must live with. On the other hand, if amid grief and loss we look to answer the "what for" question, then we find hope.

Everything doesn't happen to you! You are better off thinking there is a good reason and a purpose for everything that happens to you. Despite of how bad things may seem; all things will work for the best at the end when we walk in alignment with our purpose. God is a good and merciful God, and life is not conspiring to purposely hurt you. Whatever you do, if you are hugging the cactus, admit to the addiction, or whatever you are struggling with and confront the pain because it's time to grow.

You need to intentionally decide to take a step towards healing and growing, which encompasses conquering pain and suffering to finally be set free. For many years we have been conditioned to believe that when we face loss, we need to remain down as evidence of our love and to honor the person we lost. If we fail at a business, we are done and condemned to failure forever. That could not be further from the truth. It's not about how many times we fall, rather the ability to bounce back. That is a show of resilience, of strength, faith and of unwavering character. So, mourn and cry if you need to but don't dwell in grieving for too long. Prepare to bounce back, to learn and grow as a part of your survival.

Things to Ponder:

1. Is there a loss you never grieved and is keeping you in bondage?
2. Are you willing to let go and finally be set free?

Notes:

_____

_____

_____

_____

_____

_____

_____

_____

_____

_____

_____

_____

_____

_____

_____

_____

_____

_____

_____

_____

_____

_____

Week Two: Pain

Day Seven: *Date:*

Forgiveness is a decision that sets you free!

Reflecting on Forgiveness

Forgiveness is the best way to manifest self-love. Unforgiveness is living in bondage and will lead to bitterness. Anger and all sorts of negative emotions are aimed to destroy lives. The decision to forgive is to let go and set yourself free. You may ask yourself, "set free from what?" Set free from grudges, resentments, wounds and pain, the eagerness for revenge, and so many other negative emotions hindering our growth. You can't grow while being bound and chained to your past. A wounded heart will not grow until its healed. You will be held in a cell, captive, unable to live at your fullest. Forgiveness will heal your heart and will set you free from bondage. When you are free, then you can move on to conquer, learn and grow. Be free, fly like a free bird reaching your utmost potential.

Today, I encourage you to take a step towards freedom, by forgiving and letting go. Through this process you may remember events, things and comments that wounded your heart throughout your life. Be prompt to forgive, not just by words but forgiving deep in your heart. The perpetrators of wounds may be your parents, siblings, relatives, friends, schoolteachers, coaches, and even acquaintances you don't have contact with anymore. Understand, you DO NOT need to approach these people; this is personal, you can do this in your own intimacy. This is your decision, and the process is between you and God; you and your creator; and/or yourself and no one else. ***Do not attempt to be confrontational with whomever offended you in the past***, that will not solve anything. This is an exercise done in your intimacy, if you believe in prayer, you can pray or meditate through this process as you decide and express your forgiveness. Or you may just speak to your intimate self, and let go of the grudges, the pain, and don't hold back in letting go. You may also want to consider forgiving the person you would never think would induce you pain, yourself! Yes, forgive yourself for all the bad decisions, the losses, failed attempts, bad habits and all the negative things that you keep looking back on.

Take note: Forgiveness and Restoration are two different independent processes. Forgiveness is letting go, and restoration is reestablishing a broken or lost relationship. You may forgive, but still decide **not** to reestablish the relationship. That is perfectly fine. That is your decision and must be respected. Restoration can only happen if the offender initiates the process. They must be willing to heal and grow as well.

Things to Ponder:

Forgiveness Exercise: (This is an ongoing process and may take more than one attempt. If you feel you want to work on forgiveness for more than one day, for the sake of healing, do so. Make sure you journal through the process).

You need to take a journey deep inside your heart and dig deep to uproot the pain and what caused the wound in the first place. Once that is established, then you can make a conscious decision to forgive. If you have a hard time visualizing forgiveness, pretend you have the person you are forgiving in front of you. Set a chair and imagine the person is sitting in front of you, then you can open your heart and fully express your pain as if the person was there with you. It may seem silly, but it works. Tell them, "I forgive you for ......
(whatever wounded your heart). Simply list the things you are forgiving. As wounds are specific, so is forgiveness. Wounds and pain are not a generic event, it is specific, therefore forgiveness must be specific too. You will know you have forgiven when you remember situations and it no longer hurts. You live through experiences, and it no longer triggers negative emotions. (Garcia, 2017) When the pain is gone, you know you have healed.

Notes: Today I decide to forgive (name)_____

List the actions to forgive for every person who has offended you in the past:

(Repeat for each action and person you need to forgive)

Day one   *Date:*

Refusing change leads to stagnation

Embracing Change

E mbrace change! Your decision to start this journal shows you're seeking for change. You want to take the steps necessary to give your life a different twist, to experience higher levels of success, and reach fulfillment. Change takes effort and for this reason very many people avoid change. They rather live life with minimal effort and stay comfortable where they are. The problem with this attitude is it will never get you anywhere good and will sabotage your moving forward. If you are reaching for a higher level, if you want to succeed, then you must be ready to embrace change.

You may have heard the meaning of insanity is doing the same thing repeatedly and expecting different results. Allow the change you are embracing be the door to your sanity. Think about it for a little while here! By doing the same repeated tasks, good or bad, you have conditioned yourself to your habits, your attitude, your mindset, and if you continue in that path without change, you will stay on the hamster wheel for the rest of your life. That is insane! Is that the life you want to live? Or do you want a life of freedom, and fulfillment?

We have been conditioned throughout our lives by the things we have experienced. We have been pruned by bad and good experiences, the things we have heard, declarations spoken over our lives, listening to a constant "No, don't do that, you can't, it won't work, you will fail, you will never make it…" We hear "NO" much more than we hear "YES" in our upbringing. Do yourself a favor, don't beat yourself up about it because it is not entirely your fault. There is hope and with this journal, you will be able to change all of that.

Things to Ponder:

1. What changes have you implemented thus far that have pushed you forward?
2. How have you progressed these past two weeks?
3. Is there anything you can call a win so far in the process?

Notes:

_____

_____

_____

_____

_____

_____

_____

_____

_____

_____

_____

_____

_____

_____

_____

_____

_____

_____

_____

_____

_____

_____

_____

Week Three: Change

Day Two: *Date:*

Motivation gets you started; Discipline keeps you focused.

Motivation

Motivation is individual in nature, and its different for everyone. What motivates you, may be a turn-off for someone else. Motivation and discipline are not one in the same, yet they are both important because they complement each other. Your motivation is what pumps you up, what gets you out of bed every morning, it's what helps you start a task. You know you are motivated when you are fired up about something. Motivation is the driving force that pushes you forward to get things done. You know you are motivated when you can do something effortlessly without having to fight to take action, start a task or work on a project. To know your motivation, you need to identify your internal drive. Motivation is an important ingredient of your why, and your purpose. Knowing the source of your motivation is key to your personal and professional development. Identifying what motivates you is not enough; you must also nurture it!

To keep yourself motivated you need create the right environment by surrounding yourself with like-minded people. You must create a nurturing environment to keep the fire going. Think of yourself as a charcoal brisket in a fire. If you keep the briskets together, they will keep the fire going, but if you separate one brisket from the pile it will soon lose power thus, cooling off completely. The same concept applies to our lives. To keep yourself motivated you must surround yourself with people who inspire you not people who will distract you. People who will lift you up, not keep you down. You need to surround yourself with people who will help you remain motivated and pumped up. The coal brisket must remain in the pile to retain the fire. Your environment is important to nurture your growth. Be intentionally selective of who you allow to be part of your inner circle!

Let's identify your motivation in life and find how you will keep the fire going.

Things to Ponder:

1.What keeps you motivated?
2. What gets you up every morning?

Notes:

_____

_____

_____

_____

_____

_____

_____

_____

_____

_____

_____

_____

_____

_____

_____

_____

_____

_____

_____

_____

_____

_____

Week Three: Change

Day Three: *Date:*

Work your strengths, hire your weakness!

Strengths and Weaknesses

For many years education has been based on conquering and overcoming weaknesses. The aim was to create well-rounded professionals. However, not enough emphasis is placed in developing talents and gifts from strengths. Rather, for generations we have been taught to focus on improving our weak spots. The result has fallen short. The education system is not nearly where we want it to be at 18 years of age, when graduating from Highschool. Mainly, education standards do not match market expectations.

You can potentially reach high level outcome at whatever you decide to do, provided you work from your strengths not your weakness. On the other hand, you can spend all your life working at getting better at something you are not good at, and at best reach an average mediocre level of performance. Identifying your strengths and weaknesses is key to success. When you do something, you enjoy doing, and something you are good at it will lead you to discovering a passion you may have never identified before.

These are some Strengths and Weaknesses to consider:

Strengths	Weaknesses
Action-Oriented	Disorganized/Passive
Collaborative	Perfectionist
Accepting/Tolerant	Highly critical/Intolerant
Determined	Doubtful
Empathetic	Disagreeable/Hostile
Enthusiastic	Uninterested
Driven	People pleaser
Honest	Dishonest

Things to Ponder:

1. Let's start by identifying your strengths and weaknesses:

Exercise: Make a list below of your strengths on the left and weaknesses on the right. You are not competing, so just be honest with yourself.

Strengths	Weaknesses

1. Which of your strengths or weaknesses are you using at what you do, your profession, or career?
2. What changes can you implement to maximize the use of your strengths and /or delegate your weakness to maximize your potential?

Notes:

_____

_____

_____

_____

_____

_____

_____

_____

_____

_____

_____

_____

_____

_____

_____

_____

_____

_____

_____

_____

_____

_____

_____

_____

_____

_____

Day Four: Date:

Investment brings value!

Recognizing Your Potential and Your Self Worth

Why do so many people fail to reach their potential? Typically, it's because they **don't know** their potential, and they **don't recognize** their worth. They don't know themselves enough to recognize what they can deliver and don't really know how far they can reach. Tragically the education system promotes completion of tasks rather than talent focused education, where passing, and getting a degree is prioritized instead of leading the person to reaching their potential. Potential is filled with hope, with good vibes, promises, faith, positive energy, and fulfillness. If you want to have a chance at reaching your utmost potential, you can start by recognizing what you have to offer, and what you bring to the negotiating table. Know that reaching your potential includes being highly intentional about your growth and your future.

Growth doesn't happen by accident; it is one hundred percent intentional. You must want to grow and therefore take the steps to experience growth. One thing is true, to grow requires work. To develop yourself you must engage with the right people, create the right environment, and adopt the right habits to spur your growth. An important step in reaching your potential is discovering your skill set and recognizing your value.

Your skill set lies within your strengths. Working from your strengths will help you reach the potential your skillset offers. Your skill set is unique, so stop comparing yourself to others! You are a unique individual with virtues exclusive to you. Your virtues and talents are yours and only yours. It is also your responsibility to develop them. Being aware of your potential will help you determine the little tweaks you need to make in your behavior, implement changes that when compounded, will lead you to transformational change. Just focus on the little things you do daily, with intentionality and before you know it that "change" you seek so much, will happen with no announcement.

46

Things to Ponder:

1. Write a list of past accomplishments in your life? All kinds, any kinds…something or somethings you have accomplished that have made you proud to accomplish. Keep in mind the things you enjoy doing.

2. Out of this list of accomplishments, which are the things you enjoyed doing the most?

Notes:

_____

_____

_____

_____

_____

_____

_____

_____

_____

_____

_____

_____

_____

_____

_____

_____

_____

_____

_____

_____

_____

_____

_____

Week Three: Change

Day Five   *Date:*

It's very inexpensive to give a compliment.

-Joyce Meyer

Recognizing Your Wins

It is necessary to recognize accomplishments and give some type of recognition for reaching goals. Taking periodic breaks from your busy day to think about what has been checked off the to-do list will provide a boost of energy. There is nothing more draining than thinking you have been busy yet have accomplished nothing to move forward. Give a compliment to yourself, do it to others and get in the habit of celebrating the wins because you are worth it.

Every week, take some reflection time to meditate on what you have learned and accomplished during the week even if its little wins. Win are wins, no matter how small. You will reflect and celebrate throughout this journal, hopefully it will create the habit of doing so as you move forward. Setting some time off to meditate on your progress and growth is important to keep you on track and motivated. Avoid burnout by taking time to recognize your wins and think of ways you can improve as you recognize your efforts.

Things to Ponder:

1. Meditate on each accomplishment you listed yesterday.
2. What lessons did you learn from each accomplishment?
3. How has each accomplishment changed your life's perspective?

Take more than one day in this day module if you need to. Elaborate as needed.

Notes:

_____

_____

_____

_____

_____

_____

_____

_____

_____

_____

_____

_____

_____

_____

_____

_____

_____

_____

_____

_____

_____

_____

_____

_____

_____

_____

_____

Week Three: Change

Day Six   *Date*

Expectations is an element of faith!

Expectations

Expectations stem from mere performance and what you believe will be the outcome of events. With outcome in mind, these expectations will determine the behavior we adopt. We can experience disappointment if things don't turn out as expected, therefore any level of detachment from what's anticipated will lead to frustration and distress. This detachment may result in the inability to express gratitude, a negative attitude known to create stress and diminishing happiness.

Expectations are somehow connected to hope and faith. Because we can't give a secular definition to a spiritual word, we will go to scripture where we find the best definition of faith. Faith is defined as "the assurance of things hoped for, the conviction of things not seen" (Hebrews 11:1-HSBV). From this passage we conclude faith is the confidence and trust in what is to come. It is natural to have some type of expectations however, the expectation must have some level of congruency. The assurance of what is to come creates energy which extends towards the outcome. Faith is the currency of the supernatural and action is the currency of the natural realm. If expectations align with its corresponding action, expectations have a safe sense of reality. Action is the connecting force of faith to reality. Faith is dead without action. For example, when you start a business, you expect the business to thrive provided you make the right moves and do the right things for it to prosper. An athlete goes into a match expecting to win provided they train properly and give it their all at the court/field. Truth is, without action, faith is just an empty hope.

You can't control people's actions. Therefore, in relationships we have a high chance of disillusionment. In a relationship you need to be yourself if you want to give any relationship a fair chance for it to work long term. You expect certain behaviors from people and if you don't receive what you expect you will be disappointed. In relationships, no matter what level of relationship, it is better to be accepting than expectant. You should not "expect" changes, however they may be welcomed as the relationship prospers. Don't expect people to change for you. If there is no conviction, there will be no transformation.

The key stems from who or what are we expecting outcome. If you can control the action, you can have expectations; but if the actions are beyond your control, then expectations will have a disconnect from reality. You can control the actions you take in a business; the athlete can control the actions they take when training, and while you have a certain level of control on the actions you take, you can't control what other people do. Be careful on who or what you deposit your faith, your hopes, and expectations. Don't expose yourself to disillusionment.

Things to Ponder:

1. What expectations do you have for your life, personal growth, your job, for the next 12 months?

Notes:

_____

_____

_____

_____

_____

_____

_____

_____

_____

_____

_____

_____

Week Three: Change

Day Seven   Date:

Reflection leads to learning.

Day of Reflection

We all need a day to pause. Even God took a day off to rest after the creation. We must take a day to rest and recharge as well. Recharging is necessary, you need to stop, review, and learn from experiences.

Thus, take this day to reflect on what you have learned these past weeks and think of ways you can apply what you have learned thus far with this journal. Go back and read your notes, read some of the day's lessons and see what you can add and how you can add value to yourself moving forward. Be intentional with your personal and professional growth. It is important to learn along this journey, but more importantly is to apply what you have learned. I hear people say that "Knowledge is power". I beg to differ, I say **"Applied knowledge is Power!"** You can be knowledgeable, but if knowledge is not applied it will rot and go to waste.
So be ready to apply what you learn. Do not let it rot and go to waste. Put your knowledge to good and productive use!

Things to Ponder:

1. Go back and review the week's lessons and point out your daily takeaways.
2. What are the important lessons you have for every day this week?
3. Think of what you can do to implement your daily takeaways. This is your first step to transformation.

Notes:

Week Four: Adding Value

Day One   Date:

Adding Value is intentional giving.

My Added Value

Adding value is an intentional action. To add value to yourself and others you must be intentional about giving. There are special ingredients in this intentionality. For example, having a good and positive attitude may ignite change in someone who is feeling down and out. A smile may add value to someone's bad day. I challenge you to try it, you may be surprised at how the expression on someone's face will change from a frown to a spontaneous smile just because you smiled at them. Giving an enthusiastic good morning can change the vibe of a group. A word of encouragement, or affirmation may turn someone's day or life around. Don't fall short in giving, be intentional and make giving a part of you every day. Live with this principle in mind: what you sow, is what you reap!

Have you ever surprised someone with a cup of coffee to brighten their morning? Or even indulge their taste buds with their favorite treat? Or maybe send a caring message to a loved one, just because? The little things we do may have more value to people than pricey things. In addition, when you intentionally pay attention to your surroundings and become aware of your environment, you may get the opportunity to tend to someone in need. It does not have to be money, it could just be a word of hope, a five-minute conversation to hear someone out, or even sharing your lunch at work with someone who forgot their lunch at home. Don't release the critic that may come to judge, or to strike someone's misfortune by making things worse, keep that critic strapped and give yourself the chance to splatter good seeds!

You have gifts and talents people may need at one given point. Be prompted to share your gifts and talents. Perhaps you may give someone assistance at work if required. Don't go to the extreme of neglecting your own work, but if you can collaborate to improve the overall performance of the office, or team just do so. Focus on your personal and professional work and let your knowledge flow to the people around you. Remember, what you sow is what you reap. The seeds you sow will determine your harvest. Therefore, if you don't like the harvest, change your seeds, and make sure to sow on fertile soil. Prepare to add value to yourself as you add value to others. It will reciprocate! Life is a boomerang, what you throw will always come back.

Things to Ponder:

1. Now that you are aware of your gifts and talents, ask yourself, "what can I do to add and give value to myself and to others?"
2. How can you be more intentional in adding value to those around you and to yourself?

Notes:

_____

_____

_____

_____

_____

_____

_____

_____

_____

_____

_____

_____

_____

_____

_____

_____

_____

Week Four: Adding Value

Day Two: *Date:*

Do not compare someone's abilities,

and strengths to your flaws and weakness.

Comparison

D o you have the tendency to compare yourself to others? Don't fall in the trap of using other's accomplishments as a measure of your success. You are unique in your own way, don't look at other pastures and compare them to yours. Instead, if you concentrate on watering and fertilizing your own lawn, it may just be as beautiful and greener than the rest. You must learn how to recognize your uniqueness and value it.

We have spent the past few days reviewing and meditating on your accomplishments, wins and expectations. You now should have a clear picture of your gifts and talents. You can now use your strengths to excel in whatever you do. Now that you see your potential more clearly, can you see ways you can blossom?

Every day is a gift, and it gives you a chance to accomplish something significant, one day at a time. Something of great significance in your life is the judgment you make on yourself. Often, we are our worst critic. Your mindset can be the villain in your own story capable of sabotaging your own success. The way you think will determine the outcome on everything you do. A positive mindset will attract good results. It will open doors and pathways to reaching what you want. The opinion you have of yourself sets the standard for what happens around you.

Think about this, you can be bigger and greater than those you have been comparing yourself to. Recognize your genuine value, then you will see you are worth the investment. You have been uniquely designed to accomplish your purpose.

Decide today to set aside time and effort to grow to your highest potential. Growth takes some type of action, for instance reading the right books, attending seminars, listening to podcasts is a great way to spur personal growth. You need to set aside time to invest in yourself if you want to give yourself a chance to grow. You either value yourself or you value others over yourself. It's your choice! So, what's going be?

Recognize who you are and who you want to be…. then reach for your highest potential and work to become the ideal you.

Things to Ponder:

1. Do you find yourself comparing yourself to other people? Keep in mind that other people's accomplishments should motivate you, not bring you down.
Think of something you do well that some people may wish they did as good as you do (Make a list).
2. Embrace a positive opinion of yourself. Every morning give yourself words of affirmation to raise your self-perception.
3. Make affirmation post-it notes and put them around your computer screen, bathroom mirror etc., or a conspicuous place you won't miss.

Give yourself a promotion! ☺

Notes:

_____

_____

_____

_____

_____

_____

_____

Week Four: Adding Value

Day Three   Date

Discipline will bridge you to goals and accomplishments.

Discipline

New Year resolutions are the thing every year. Many people make them, but not many keep them. That is very unfortunate because goals are to be met, and everyone should have them. One of the most common New Year's resolutions is joining a gym to "get in shape", or maybe "lose weight". Others may have business related goals such as, "increase their income", "get a new job" or even "start a business". The point is that most everyone has New Year's resolutions or set goals during the year. The question is, are those goals met? You need to be convicted towards meeting your goals. How bad do you want them?

Even though you may be motivated to do something, without discipline you will never get anything done. Motivation will get the engine started, but discipline will keep it in motion. You may join the gym, but that alone will not get you fit. All you will accomplish is having an added expense and it will end at that. Most people end up quitting for lack of discipline. If you don't have the discipline to persist on going to the gym consistently and persist on accomplishing the daily process regardless of how you feel, you will get nowhere close to reaching your goal. You need discipline in school to be in class on time, read the material, study, start, and finish projects to meet expectations. You need discipline to get up every morning early to plan for your new business, follow through persistently even though you see no immediate results. You need discipline to implement a way to reach set goals, otherwise it will remain just a goal, a dream, a vision…. unrealized with no accomplishments.

What makes the difference between people who make it happen and those who don't? For one, a desire on fire will work wonders. You need conviction, to want it bad enough. Second, you need to discipline yourself to make it happen. One of the biggest deterrents in reaching goals is setting expectations and goals too far off your reach and that will dry down the fire of motivation. Especially if you are not in the right environment for proper nourishment.

Light up that fire! Think in terms of small steps rather than big steps that may seem unreachable. Remember, motivation gets you **on** task, discipline keeps you **in** the task.

You need to think in terms of what you **must** do, not what you **feel like** doing. If you leave it up to your emotions, you will not accomplish much. Keep your eyes on the target and push yourself until your reach it. Feelings have no bearing on goals, it's not about what you feel, it's what you must do. The right attitude will get you to accomplish your goals. Stretch yourself off your comfort zone and get off the couch!

Things to Ponder:

1. What are you struggling with right now, something you have tried before but have not been able to accomplish?
2. Are you ready to commit to doing what you must to accomplish what you want?

Notes:

_____
_____
_____
_____
_____
_____
_____
_____
_____
_____
_____

_____

_____

_____

_____

_____

_____

_____

_____

_____

_____

_____

_____

_____

_____

_____

_____

_____

_____

_____

_____

_____

_____

_____

_____

_____

_____

_____

Week Four: Adding Value

Day Four   *Date:*

Discipline is the bridge between goals and accomplishments.

Consistent small steps will lead to big strides.

Consistency

Taking small steps in accomplishing goals, will take you further than trying to accomplish too much at once. Trying to do too much will seem too daunting of a task and will lead to overwhelm and finally disappointment. Therefore, reaching small realistic goals will lead you to consistent wins and as a result, motivating you to stay on task. The strategy of a marathon runner is much different than a sprinter. Life is a marathon, not a sprint. Thus, you need to implement a strategy like that of a marathon runner not a sprinter. Consistent running with a steady pace will get the runner further than stretching yourself to lead the pack and establishing the pace for the whole race. You may end up losing your energy and ultimately falling further behind risking not having enough stamina to finish the race.

What does this tell you? Its ok to have long term goals while concentrating on short term accomplishments, smaller steps that if followed through consistently will take you to longer distances. These smaller steps which I call milestones, if applied consistently, will take you to cross the finish line succeeding at obtaining the bigger long-term goals that once seemed too far out of reach. Breaking the long-term goal down into reachable milestones will keep you motivated as you reach short-term goals. Do please celebrate your wins as you reach the bigger goals. That is a boost of energy to keep you motivated.

Student syndrome is waiting for the last minute to cram or complete an assignment, project, or goal. If you appreciate high quality work, waiting for last minute will never work in reaching excellence. On the other hand, focusing on small daily tasks will help you build discipline and consistency in all you do. Accomplishing milestones will help you build your morale. It will boost your self-confidence and give you a more consistent sense of accomplishment. Even if your small wins seem insignificant, by the mere actions of doing what you said you would do will be enough to give you a boost of feeling accomplished and that unconsciously will feed on your self-confidence.

Build your to do list one day at a time, accomplish milestones each day by checking tasks off your daily to-do list. What you don't finish one day, make sure to move it for next day. Do not forget to prioritize your "to-do's" and stick with your list. Don't get distracted and stay focused on what needs to be done. Block your schedule on top priorities. Get ready to celebrate your weekly wins because you will inevitably accomplish goals by the end of the week by focusing on small milestone daily goals. Implement a daily to do list and make sure to check off tasks accomplished. Review your performance every end of the week and measure your progress moving forward. Do celebrate your wins, write down the things accomplished and give yourself some credit. Celebrate yourself and celebrate your wins!

Things to Ponder:

1. Task: Break down you goals into milestones (small steps) and implement the milestone concept by setting realistic reachable small steps to accomplish a bigger goal.
2. What is one thing you have not been able to conquer and accomplish that you would like to reach right now? Are you up to the challenge? Yes, or No?

Notes:

_____

_____

_____

_____

_____

_____

_____

Week Four: Adding Value

Day Five   Date:

Quitting is not an option!

Perseverance

Perseverance is the ability to persist despite of circumstance. To continue during negative circumstances may appear as a daunting task, but the alternative will not make things better or any easier. Quitting is not an option winners consider. That is what sets winners and losers apart, perseverance is a key ingredient to accomplishment and success. The only thing guaranteed when you give up is never accomplishing your goals. Is that what you want? Know you will fail sometime, and we all do. The key to success is having the ability to stumble, fall and getting up as many times as required to reach set goals. There is no burden heavy enough to keep you down.

You need to grow strong and focused on what needs to be done. Never lose sight of your goals. Adjust if you must but get up and set the pace forward. The best way out of a situation is seeing it through. You must be determined to hit your target, and nothing should stand in your way of accomplishing it. Not trying is far worse than failure. Failure is a temporary situation, not trying is the permanent dismantling of your dreams.

Far too many people give up inches away from hitting their goals. Your will and determination must be stronger than discouragement, criticism, and negativity around you. Be mentally prepared to deal with all the negatives you will confront along the way. Your eyes need to be set on your goals and not the storm. The storm will pass, and clear skies will soon approach. Insist to persist on what you have set yourself to do. Work the muscle of persistence, build it by reminding yourself of the goals you have set. Take one day at a time focusing on the milestones, on the daily tasks. Accomplished milestones will compound with time and soon enough you will see big results. Implement the eye of the tiger strategy. They set their eyes on their prey, and they don't let go until they catch it. Stay focused and never give up!

If you are ever tempted to give up, remember what motivated you to set the goal or goals in the first place. Sometimes you need to go back to basics and remind yourself of what set the fire in you. Adjust if you may, but don't ever quit!

Things to Ponder:

1. Have you given up on something you have always wanted to do?
2. Why did you give up? Lack of discipline, or motivation?
3. Do you consider yourself a persistent person? Or do you tend to give up without a fight when things get tough? If you do, how often do you give up?

Notes:

_____

_____

_____

_____

_____

_____

_____

_____

_____

_____

_____

_____

_____

_____

_____

_____

Week Four: Adding Value

Vision and Mission

Vision is aspirational and inspiring; it is a statement that motivates people towards long term goals. Businesses have a vision statement, why don't you? You need to create a short and concise statement that will inspire you toward your long-term goals. Short term goals are goals set to be accomplished within 12 months. Intermediate goals within 2-5 years and long-term beyond the five-year mark.

Have you ever thought where and who you would like to be in 10 years? What are the things you would like to accomplish on the long-term? Many people confuse the vision and the mission, and they are very different. The vision is aimed to the future, and it's focused on long-term goals. It inspires customers and stakeholders on issues they may care about. It describes how you see yourself, your business and how you and your business will add value to the world. It should include your contribution to society.

Mission, on the other hand, focuses on short-term goals, and are the steps required to reaching the vision. It is the how, the who, the where and the why you will achieve the vison or its objectives. It is not inspirational, rather it is action oriented. It is your roadmap, your action plan to reach the vision and its long-term goals.

When writing your vision statement, you must be ambitious. Think big! While being realistic at the same time. Without ambition you can't plan for growth. Work on a financial projection you can follow. It must also reflect your values. You will not be motivated if it goes against the values you want to pursue. It must also be inspirational, to employees, stakeholders, customers, and vendors. The vision statement should be displayed so people feel connected. Your vision statement should reflect your purpose. Once you write your vision statement make sure it is clear for the public to understand, it is inspiring, and it can be easily remembered.

Things to Ponder:

1. Prepare a vision board if you like art. If not, brainstorm, write several examples and then start combining and/or eliminating until you get to your final vision statement.
2. Write your vision in a place you see every day. Remember you need to allow time for gestation. It takes time to develop.

Notes:

_____

_____

_____

_____

_____

_____

_____

_____

_____

_____

_____

_____

_____

My Vision Statement:

_____

_____

_____

_____

_____

Week Four: Adding Value

Day Seven: Date:

"Reflective thinking turns experience into insight."
– John C. Maxwell

Day of Reflection

A day to reflect is a day to meditate on past experiences and learned lessons. We can't go through life's experiences without a learned lesson. Life experiences are opportunities to grow. Life is a training session. We are training every day and we train to get better, to perform better and to grow as a result.

Take this day to reflect on the lessons you learned these past four weeks. Meditate on how you applied the things you discovered and learned about yourself and others. Review the recorded changes that have added value to your life so far.

Remember there is value in reviewing, meditating, and planning. Invest your time today in going over what you have done thus far during this "Flip the Switch! to a Better You" journal challenge to establish yourself and your accomplishments.

Things to ponder:

1. Reflect on what you have learned this past week.
2. Meditate on the daily takeaways.
3. What changes can you implement to capitalize on lessons learned?
......then celebrate wins!

Notes:

_____

_____

_____

_____

_____

_____

_____

_____

_____

_____

_____

_____

_____

_____

_____

_____

_____

_____

_____

_____

_____

_____

_____

_____

_____

Week Five: Goal Setting

The sniper's success lies on the accuracy to hit the target.

Setting Goals

Setting goals provide a roadmap to reaching what you have envisioned. There are short-term and long-term goals, and they are both important. Short-term goals are those you have set to accomplish within the next 12 months, and long-term goals are those you set for over a 12-month period.

You must strategize goal setting to increase the chances of attainability. There are key ingredients in goal setting we will review this week.

Goals must be:
1. **Specific**
2. **Measurable**
3. **Attainable**
4. **Realistic**
5. **Target Date**

This is the strategy to follow to setting goals that will lead to wins. Wins will help you keep your motivation on fire and discipline will see you through the finish line.

Things to Ponder:

1. List any goals you have established but never reached?
2. What goals or dreams do you have that you would like to accomplish?
3. Think of short and long-term goals you would like to set now to reach your dreams.

Notes:

_____

_____

_____

_____

_____

_____

_____

_____

_____

_____

_____

_____

_____

_____

_____

_____

_____

_____

_____

_____

_____

_____

_____

_____

_____

_____

_____

_____

Week Five: Goal Setting

Goals must be Specific.

Goals need to be focused and specific. You need to know exactly what you need to accomplish. If a goal is vague, you will be unable to focus your energy on accomplishing it. It must be specific enough that you will clearly see the path and recognize when it is accomplished.

Again, a sniper's success is in the ability to aim at a specific target and shoot accurately to hit it with precision. You need to properly identify your target to pursue it. Obscured or blurred targets are difficult to hit. Improve your likelihood of wins by setting goals that are specific, that you can envision, that you can own. Without a specific destination it's difficult to plan a trip. You need to know exactly where you are going to specify what route to take. Taking any route will lead you nowhere. The more specific your destination, the more likely it is the arrival.

Set specific goals that you understand, and that you will easily recognize when accomplished.

Things to Ponder:

1. Think of ways you can make the goals you thought of yesterday more specific and recognizable today.
2. Revisit them and adjust them as you see fit. Be specific!

Notes:

Week Five: Goal Setting

Day Three   *Date:*

If you can measure it, you can accomplish it!

Goals must be Measurable

When setting your goals, be mindful of ways you can measure your progress. Without measuring performance there is no way to monitor progress. If you don't establish ways to monitor and measure progress, you can't establish methods of improving thus you will lose track of your goals. Your target may be way off your range, and without you even realizing it your goal may drift further away from your reach.

Measuring your progress will help you adjust your plan of action when required, while reaching your target as expected. For instance, imagine you are traveling to a distant city. For you to make traveling plans you need to know what the distance is to travel and the time you have available to reach your destination. You can then plan accordingly and set the amount of distance you need to travel per day to reach your destination on time. You need to measure your traveled distance at the end of every traveling day to reach your destination at the desired time. This is how you keep your plans on target thus accomplishing your goals without delay.

Things to Ponder:

1. Find a way to measure your plan's progress. Make sure you can easily monitor performance to keep you focused and on target. Write it down and keep it simple.
2. Keep milestones clear and keep you daily goals
3. Can you recognize and prove when goals have been completed?

Notes:

_____

_____

_____

_____

_____

_____

_____

_____

_____

_____

_____

_____

_____

_____

_____

_____

_____

_____

_____

_____

_____

_____

_____

_____

_____

_____

Week Five: Goal Setting

Goals must be Attainable.

For goals to be attainable, you must be able to control the actions that will lead to accomplishing them. The actions can't be beyond your control otherwise you will be unable to design an action plan that will work. This is the reason goals must be specific because vague goals are unattainable. They are loose and unstable; therefore, you will have no grasp, much less precision to aim and target them. Goals must be attainable otherwise they will remain a dream, something you wish for but not within your reach. You must go step by step. Stay on target and make it real.

Let me illustrate an example so you have an idea of what makes a goal attainable. I may wish to become professional golf player, and I love to play golf, but I must ask myself a question. Am I good at it? Good enough to make the cut? When setting goals, we must make sure it is something attainable, within my physical and mental capabilities. You need to play from your strengths, not your weakness. When setting goals make sure its within your core strengths otherwise it may qualify as a hobby, not a career or business. Do stretch yourself, but also make sure it is within your reach. Base your actions from your strengths, and delegate from your weakness.

Things to Ponder:

1. Review your goal and ask yourself if the goal is attainable. Is your plan of action something you can control?
2. Review your goals, make sure they are specific and not vague, make sure you can measure its progress and make sure it is attainable considering the resources you have available. If not, prepare to adjust as necessary. Consider smaller more attainable goals that will lead you to a more long-term goal down the line.

Notes:

Week Five: Goal Setting

Goals must be Realistic.

Setting realistic goals is not about allowing fear to intervene nor is it being negative, unbelieving or having lack of faith. Realistic goals are set to increase our chances of accomplishment. When we set goals that are too far out of reach, we find ourselves battling self-doubt and overwhelm. Instead of overreaching, think of accomplishing short-term milestones, taking small steps that eventually will take you closer to your long-term goal. Instead of struggling, break the process down into smaller more realistic, reachable steps leading you to reaching a bigger and larger goal. Implement the basic "slowly but surely" strategy. Maybe you don't have the resources yet, and that will make it too difficult to accomplish and perhaps unattainable for the moment. For that reason, smaller milestones allow you to have a clear picture of your goals. Otherwise, it will become a burden and unable to enjoy the process, which will lead you to feeling overwhelmed. So instead of changing the goal, just adjust the plan, break it down into smaller more realistic goals known as milestones. Commit to actionable milestones while not losing track of the bigger picture, and your goal.

Again, work from your strengths. In my example from yesterday, you must ask yourself if becoming a professional athlete is realistic. Do I have the resources, the time, the money to invest in coaches? Am I at age to start practicing a new discipline and be competitive? Those are the questions that must be considered in your decision. Again, it is not about being negative, or having lack of faith…it's about playing the game in a way that accounts for the resources you have available. Not everyone that enjoys playing a sport is meant to be a professional, but that doesn't mean you can't enjoy a game with some friends every so often. You must be mindful of what you have and what you can provide according to the resources you have while aiming to become better regardless of your position today. Keep in mind you always need to know where you stand, where you want to be, and who you want to become as a result.

Things to Ponder:

1. Considering your resources, is the established milestone possible? Will it lead you closer to your established goal?
2. What action will be the best use of your time and resources right now?
3. Are you committed to accomplishing the set milestones?
4. What are the main obstacles you would confront?

Notes:

_____

_____

_____

_____

_____

_____

_____

_____

_____

_____

_____

_____

_____

_____

_____

_____

_____

Week Five: Goal Setting

Day Six   *Date:*

Goals are dreams with deadlines-Diana Scharf

Goals must have a Target Date

Goal deadlines are essential to measure progress for any project. There is no real way to make a goal measurable without a well-established clear deadline. Whether a team or a solo player, deadlines are a way to keep the goals on target. Keep in mind life happens, and it may throw a curve ball at you in the form of persuasive distractions, unexpected situations, and very attractive opportunities that may get you out of track. Be aware that distractions will back-track you a bit and delay the target date for you. That is fine if you get back on the plan and follow through with it. You need to pick up your pace, get back on track and keep moving forward.

Stretching yourself will keep you challenged; however, target dates must be realistically probable. Possibility is a yes and no answer, either can it be done or not. Probability is a statistical measure and can't be answered with a simple yes or no it requires data and analysis. Target dates may also be set in range dates, from – to dates which will also provide a bit of flexibility and may take some unnecessary pressure off the table.

Goal achievement may encompass a "minimum" of sales, social media followers, new likes or a minimum of new clients signed up by a specific date. You need to establish a date to know when the goal should be at completion. Setting completion dates will allow to reverse engineer the plan and set specific actions necessary to accomplish the goals. These fixed dates may be moved but realize it can't be a habit to keep extending every time the target date is not reached. Any extension must have a purpose and reason behind it. Maybe adjustments were necessary for better results however, it can be the perfect excuse for failure.

Stay on target by accomplishing milestones, with consistency!

Things to Ponder:

1. Pick a date for each goal that is realistic yet challenging.
2. Think of setting dates for each step to keep you on track and organized.

Notes:

_____

_____

_____

_____

_____

_____

_____

_____

_____

_____

_____

_____

_____

_____

_____

_____

_____

_____

_____

_____

_____

Week Five: Goal Setting

Day Seven   *Date*

Setting goals is the first step to transforming dreams into reality.

Day of Reflection

Considering you know how to implement the five characteristics to goal setting, you are now in a better position to obtain goals for yourself. Let's consider a very common goal and put it into action:

Goal #1: Lose Weight (Example)
Specific: Lose 100 lbs.
Measurable: losing 2 lbs. a week sounds more reasonable than losing 100 lbs. A goal to lose 100 lbs. may be too daunting of a task. You will be prone to discouragement and giving the whole idea up and gaining the weight back if any accomplished.
Attainable: Losing 2 lbs. a week is completely attainable with a regimen and exercise program. Think of actions you can take to accomplish this weekly milestone. Remember, consistency is key. Aim to accomplish the milestones that will slowly take you to accomplish your goal.
Realistic: Losing 2 lbs. is completely realistic. According to experts in the field it is recommended a person to lose 1 to 2 lbs. a week as a healthy and safe program.
Target Date: Losing 2 lbs. per week means a person should lose 100 lbs. in 50 weeks. The target date should be set for 52 weeks or 1 year.

Final Goal: Lose 100 lbs. in 52 weeks.
Milestone: Losing 1 to 2 lbs. weekly

Plan: Follow exercise routine Monday-Wednesday and Friday
Walking for 10 minutes after lunch time
before going back to work
Measure weight every week-Journal your progress
Diet: Follow life changing eating habits
Monitor and set caloric or macros intake-Daily.
Habit Curbing: No fast foods | No Sugar | No processed foods
This is an example and not a nutrition plan. Speak with your doctor or nutritionist before starting a weight management or exercise program to make sure it is right for you and your health.

The purpose of this example is to give you an idea of how SMART plans are written considering all points to follow. You must now write your own SMART goals according to your needs. Goals may be financial, work related, spiritual, or personal.

Things to Ponder:

1. Write your goals down with all 5 ingredients in S-M-A-R-T goal setting. Start with long-term goals, then work into the short-term milestones.
2. How do you envision yourself in 5 years? Reverse engineer the long-term goals into smaller milestones (for the next 12 months) which in turn, will take you to accomplish the long-term goal at the end.
3. Make an action plan for each goal, set a start date, and commit to start and have the conviction to finish! You need to build the habit of finishing what you start. It is part of building discipline. Discipline is what keeps you going.

Notes:

_____

_____

_____

_____

_____

_____

_____

_____

_____

_____

_____

_____

_____

_____

_____

Week Six: Laying my Foundation

Day One   Date:

Our ability to handle life's challenges,

is a measure of our strength of character. -Les Brown

Character

Character is defined, according to Oxford Languages, as "the mental and moral qualities distinctive of an individual." Therefore, character speaks of *who we are,* and success speaks of *what we do.* Thus, *what we do can never be more important and can't take priority over who we are.* Basically, we are a combination of the two. Having character is setting our principles and values at the core center of our lives weighing morale, ethics, law, and order over any desire, goal, or financial gain we may seek. For instance, a person with character puts value in their word, their "no" means No; and their "yes" means Yes. Their words have content and are in fact reliable. Therefore, as we grow personally, we must also grow in character.

Money does not give a person character, on the flip side, you can give character to your hard-earned dollars. In essence we need to concentrate on growth rather than outcome. Don't waste your life pursuing money, like water it will somehow slip right through your fingers. Rather pursue growth and money will flow as a result. Get your priorities in order and set the values and principles which you want to live by and commit to making them your life's motto. Your values and principles have a symbolic significance as it adds character to who you are and what you represent.

Your values and principles, your character and your will are strong ingredients to the foundation by which you will ignite prosperity in your life. Everything you do has consequences, good or bad. *Your deeds are seeds and your life is a garden.* Those seeds we sow will soon germinate and grow. As you build character be sure to plant the good seed, think and speak positive, establish your principles and values as you build character. Start every morning by affirming who you are, your character, listening to words that affirm your values and never forget to express gratitude. This is who you represent, and what you will be known by.

Things to Ponder:

1. What are the traits of **your** character?
(Diagnose yourself and be brutally honest about it)
Examples: Honesty, Fairness, Humbleness, Kindness, Integrity etc.

Notes:

_____

_____

_____

_____

_____

_____

_____

_____

_____

_____

_____

_____

_____

_____

_____

_____

_____

_____

_____

Week Six: Laying my Foundation

Day Two   *Date:*

Reputation is for time; character is for eternity.

-J.B. Gough

Character Traits

Character is not the same as personality, however they are interrelated. Personality reveals your behavior, and it's an outward expression of yourself. Personality refers to a set of qualities in your behavior and attitudes manifested in your daily life.

Character, on the other hand, is a set of moral principles and standards that shape your life. It is the essence and the inward expression of who you are. These character traits trigger your emotions and thus affects how you tend to feel and how you act. It defines the patterns of your thoughts. It is what shapes your mere being and defines your choices and actions. Your character traits reflect on your core values and beliefs, it defines who you are, manifested when confronted with moral and ethical questions.

Identify your character traits and they will lead you to who you are.

These are key character traits to consider:

Generosity, integrity, loyalty, devotion, loving, caring, respectful, sincere, embracing, self-control, sound-mind, straight-forwardness, courage, integrity, compassion, honesty…(etc.). Deceiving, ambiguity, erratic, fearful, disrespectful, insincere, lack of empathy…(etc.).

Things to Ponder:

1. Which of the character traits you identified yesterday would you like to keep (traits you admire), and which traits would you like to change and or improve?

2. Name character traits you would like to build and make yours?

Notes:

_____

_____

_____

_____

_____

_____

_____

_____

_____

_____

_____

_____

_____

_____

_____

_____

_____

_____

_____

_____

_____

_____

_____

Week Six: Laying my Foundation

Day Three   *Date:*

Character is doing the right thing even when nobody's looking- J.C. Watts

---

Developing Character Traits

In the past two days you have been pondering on your character, learning what it is and diagnosing your own. You have had the opportunity to meditate on the traits of your character. These past few days should give yourself a good idea on who you really are when nobody is around. It should be clear to you, who your private self really is and how your private self is manifested as you connect with others.

Yesterday you determined which of your character traits you would like to keep, and which you would like to change. Knowing what you know about your character now, you need to determine if you are willing to take the steps to experience transformational change to build your character and become the person you would like to become. In other words, the ideal you. Today you need to decide to take additional steps towards this wonderful experience of change. Are you proud of who you are, or who have you become? Take a closer look at yourself in the mirror and ask yourself if you like who the person in the mirror represents?

Character is built and developed with time as your life experiences shape who you are, but that doesn't mean you can't intentionally take steps to improve your character traits. To do so, you must take proper steps to accomplish change and become a person of good character. Your ideal self, the person you would be proud to be. If you don't like who you are, you should commit to change!

As you take upon this challenge, you must be intentional to accomplish this most important and significant project. Your character traits will define who you are and you are about to design the person you always desired to be, but never was.

These are examples of 12-character traits you may want to pursue:

Humbleness: Being humble is being true, accepting, and teachable. Not boasting, arrogant or thinking more of yourself than others.

Honesty: Be sincere and don't mislead people. Better yet, don't breach the trust in relationships and never take anything that's not yours.

Integrity: The word integrity means all in one, not broken apart. Therefore, your mind, heart, your spirit and physical being is all one. Say what you mean and mean what you say. Don't break under pressure.

Be a promise keeper: Honor your commitments; pay what you owe, take care of what is entrusted to you and return what you borrow.

Loyalty: Stand by your own including family and friends. Promote unity and never gossip, it causes division. Hold yourself true to yourself and others.

Prudent: Be slow to speak and prompt to listen. Discipline your tongue, it's a lethal weapon.

Responsibility: Be thoughtful and consider consequences; be accountable to yourself.

Pursue excellence: Take pride in what you do and aim for the best. Don't settle for mediocracy.

Love and Kindness: Be generous and compassionate with those in need.

Respect: Treat people with courtesy, be polite and judge based on merits, accepting people for who they are. All honorable labor deserves fair compensation.

Fairness: Treat all people fairly; be understanding of people's needs and feelings.

Have a sense of community: Obey the law, respect authority, exercise your right to vote, volunteer to help, do not litter, and take care of your surroundings.

To accomplish changes, you need to be ready and committed to invest in yourself. Remember, you need to nourish growth and create value to yourself.

Developing good character traits will help you build solid friendships, and relationships. It will also enhance your career and just as importantly, it will ascertain an excellent foundation for reaching success.

Things to Ponder:

1. How important to you is your personal growth?
2. How important is liking who you are?
3. Take charge: Design the person you want to become by choosing your character traits. Commit to change, practice awareness, implement changes, and watch your transformation.

Notes:

_____

_____

_____

_____

_____

_____

_____

_____

_____

_____

_____

_____

_____

_____

_____

_____

_____

Week Six: Building my Foundation

Building Character

Building character is an intentional act. It is your choice, and you can take steps to change for the better by changing your character traits. To do this you need to be aware of the changes you desire and intentionally work to implement the changes required to experience character transformation. These are specific steps you need to take when embarking in making the changes necessary to build character:

- Be humble, you must be open to change.
- Have a clear vision of your character traits,
  they determine who you are.
- Be intentional and determined to change and transformation.
- Practice discipline, be constant to practice character traits daily.
- Be accountable, don't give up and don't give in. Focus!
- Choose your inner circle carefully, surround yourself with like-minded people who share *your new set of values*.

Be constant in practicing the traits you want to develop. You don't have to change all of them at once but choose the most relevant and concentrate on accomplishing them. Slowly implement more changes until you accomplish them all. This is a lifestyle, lifelong commitment you need to stick to. Get people around you to call things to your attention and be humble to admit when off track. Don't be embarrassed, be focused.

Character traits speak of who you are, and you must practice what you preach. Give value to your words, by doing what you say you will do. This process takes conviction and commitment. It will take time, so focus on the outcome you want, stay motivated and be disciplined to accomplish the changes you have committed to. You can't put this on the back burner and expect things to change. To build character you must have your core values always present in your daily life, it's the things you value the most. This is who you are or who you want to become. It is priority to develop change!

Things to Ponder:

1. Review the character traits you said have that you would like to change, and the traits you currently have you want to keep?
2. What things would you change or implement to establish a consistent personal growth of character?
3. What are you willing to do to strengthen your character?
4. Would you consider an accountability partner to keep you in check?

Notes:

_____

_____

_____

_____

_____

_____

_____

_____

_____

_____

_____

_____

_____

_____

_____

_____

_____

Week Six: Laying my Foundation

Day Five   *Date:*

Self -Doubt is evidence of flourishing fear.

Battling Self-Doubt

Self-doubt is a personal battle for most people, something most of us struggle with every day. Even successful people struggle with self-doubt at a given point in their lives. To overcome self-doubt, you need to take steps forward instead of freezing before challenges. It takes courage to take risks. Success is not absent of failures, and mistakes. Instead, it is the compilation of experiences, both wins and losses shaping your resilience and stamina to keep going until reaching your goals and fulfilling your calling. *Setbacks keep us humble and wins motivated.* Thus, when you face troubled times, you need to pick yourself up and try again until you get the expected results. Self-doubt is dressed in fear, and the burden of fear paralyzes. That is the one thing we can't afford to carry around.

Imagine Thomas Edison working on his invention, the light bulb, which completely changed the world for ever. He experienced failed attempt after failed attempt in the process of his invention. Do you think he was exempt of doubts? After so many tries, getting no good results, and failing repeatedly, I imagine people around him questioned his efforts and the thought of giving up must have crossed his mind more than once. However, his resilience is evident and obviously, kept going despite the negatives until he got the results he expected. The proof is in the lightbulb. Without his persistence, who knows how much longer it would have taken to come up with this bright invention we all use every day.

Don't beat yourself up for having doubts, what matters is HOW you confront self-doubt. We will start by turning doubt into confidence. You need to tame the critic living inside you and it takes practice.

Here are three strategies that will get you started:

1. Guard your self-talk by taming your tougher critic.
2. Don't follow your emotions, and
3. Continue to work on discipline.

Guard your self-talk and tame the critic. There are three voices that speak to us, the voice of God (the good angel on the one side), you may want to call it the voice of the light, or the voice of good. Then there is the voice of Evil (the dark angel on the other side) or the voice of darkness. Lastly your own voice, the critic, which is always yapping at your ear and many times it's just repeating what the dark angel is telling you, which is never good. It never delivers good news!

Our senses are filters, and you must filter everything you hear, the things you see, the things you taste and the things you touch. For instance, the words you feed your brain including the messages in music will affect your mental state and mindset. If the music you hear talks about drugs and sex, your mind will go there and soon enough you will be seeking that environment. You must filter the things you see and hear because you will hear them so many times, you will soon start believing, attracting, and pursuing it. Be careful about conversations around you, at work, among acquaintances…don't listen to garbage. Garbage in, garbage out!

Be watchful of how you speak to yourself! You will become what you repeatedly say to yourself. It's like claiming it, "I called it!" Don't be negative, instead affirm yourself with words of encouragement and motivation. Listen to words of affirmation and dismiss any bad vibes that come your way. Not comingling with negative people is a good start. Negativity is contagious, so cast it out!

Things to Ponder:

1. Are you aware of your inner critic? Are you aware of its voice? Can you recognize it?
2. Does your inner voice relentlessly punish you? Is it a constant put down? How much does it influence your character traits?

3. Can you commit to tame this beast? Tame your inner voice, train your mind to thinking encouragement. Be aware of your principles and values. Listen to words of affirmation, or perhaps bible promises that will surely lift your spirits.

Notes:

_____

_____

_____

_____

_____

_____

_____

_____

_____

_____

_____

_____

_____

_____

_____

_____

_____

_____

_____

_____

Week Six: Laying my Foundation

Day Six   Date:

You're busy doubting yourself while others
are intimidated by your full potential.

Overcoming Self-Doubt

Self-doubt is a bad habit shaped by your life experiences. It is not something we are born with; we are confident from birth; however, our confidence is slowly broken by our experiences as we grow up. A baby is confident that their needs will be met. Most often, they call out in the only way they know, and they are tended for. However, by the time we become adults, our confidence is undermined by experiences, opinions, and comments we constantly hear. Without a doubt, our life's experiences affect how we perceive our environment and the people around us.

The strongest influences in our lives are from the people closest to us, our parents, siblings, family, teachers, and friends. Incidentally, these are precisely the people we spend the most time with inside and outside our home. Since childhood, we are like sponges absorbing from experiences that shape the way we think, the way we act, react, respond to situations and consequently, the way we feel. Hence, the influence our environment and the people around us have in our lives shapes who we become.

We also crave unconditional love and affection, and when we are starved, we grow needy, and become people pleasers. As such, to earn the love and affection we so much crave, we become what we think they want us to be instead of who we are. Remember, these are just perceptions, and perceptions are most often disconnected from the truth and reality. You must reprogram your chip and eliminate the bugs planted in your head from childhood to adulthood. These bugs are responsible for forming those undesirable limiting beliefs that cripple your growth. Its time to flip the switch to a better you!

You need to reprogram yourself and your mindset. Reprograming requires feeding your brain with new information about yourself. It's like purging a file and saving another in its place. Therefore, it's so important to filter through everything you hear because it will influence your mindset. Your senses are filters to your brain. If you hear negative things the impact those words will have in your life will be negative. Thus, surround yourself with positive company, listen to music with positive messages, words of affirmation and encouragement. Read personal development books that feeds to your growth. Remember to be intentional about growth, don't leave it to chance. It is unequivocally your choice.

The environment you live in will either nurture you or starve you. The circle you engage with is a determining factor in your growth. A seed will never grow in soil that lacks nutrients. It will soon wither never reaching its potential. Make sure to stand on fertile ground. Be intentional in how you perceive yourself and what you are capable of accomplishing. This will manifest in your life with great influence in outcome. Never surrender the control of your life to an external factor other than God.

Things to Ponder:

1. Take a good transparent look at the environment you are in. Ask yourself sincerely, ...Is my environment fertile soil I can blossom and grow??
2. Is my environment nurturing? Is it fertile soil? Or do I have better chances if I change my environment?

Exercise: Think about what influence you are receiving from your environment, from the people around you and what is your inner self feeding you?

Examples: If your environment if of bad influence, change it! Get new friends, maybe you would want to let go of the circle of friends altogether.

If all you hear is "You are no good", "how stupid of you", "you are such a failure", "it is not possible" .... Whichever it is, write them down, and make a list. Next to each phrase, write an action you can take to neutralize the critical phrase. Turn the negative around and tell yourself what you need to do to make sure you neutralize all negative messages.

Don't let it become a self-fulfilling prophecy. Practice it daily so you can learn to neutralize the inner critic's messages. So, every time the inner critic's voice appears, you will remind yourself of the neutralizing words and repeat them to yourself. You will hear the neutralizing words until you believe it. Your commitment throughout the day is to be AWARE of the inner critic's voice and to be prompt to turning it around and taking steps to prove the inner critic wrong. You must exercise this throughout the day, until you learn to tame it. The trick is to keep it under your control because if you let it lose, its intention is to manipulate and sabotage your success. Don't leave your future at the mercy of external forces. You have the power to turn things around!

Notes:

_____

_____

_____

_____

_____

_____

_____

_____

_____

_____

_____

_____

_____

_____

_____

_____

_____

_____

Week Six: Laying my Foundation.

Day Seven   *Date:*

Self-reflection may be scary, but necessary for growth.

Day of Reflection

O ne advantage to reflection is learning from past mistakes. If you don't take time to look back to review your decisions, wins, and mistakes you may fail to learn from past experiences. Particularly, mistakes teach us important lessons you may not want to repeat. Mistakes can be important learning tools that spur growth. You learn more from failures than you do from wins. So, it is important to capitalize on failures as well as you do on wins. Time of reflection will help you do exactly that and it is an important step in the learn and grow process.

Reflect on what you have learned during the past few days about the foundational pillars you have built in your life. Also reflect on how you can turn the old, encrypted messages you had been fed, and turn them into new positive uplifting messages to make significant wins instead of failures.

Things to Ponder:

1. How have you progressed this week?
2. What changes have you implemented that have pushed you forward?

Notes:

_____

_____

_____

_____

_____

Week Seven: Emotions

Day One   *Date*

It's not what I feel, it's what I do that matters.

What are Emotions?

Emotions are an expression of released energy. Our actions are energy; therefore, actions release the energy that create emotions, not the other way around. It's only logical! You can't allow your emotions to guide your actions. If you do, your decisions would be based on how you feel, and feelings are not a solid foundational pillar to base decisions on. That can be very dangerous. Decisions should be based on the analysis of data and information, not on feelings.

To help you conquer the battle between reason and feelings. For example, you need to program your mind not to make decisions while in a vulnerable emotional state. Repeat to yourself, "It's not what I feel, it's what I do that matters". At the end of the day the right actions are followed by its identifying emotion. So, don't wait to feel good to do things, rather take action to alter your emotions and feel good as a result. Take the actions that will produce the energy to create the emotions you want to experience thus, leading you to feel the way want to feel. Feeling good will create the right environment to set yourself in a good state of mind. You should refrain from making decisions until your emotions are normalized and under control. This routine will help you avoid problems and will help you make better and more wise decisions in the future.

Keep in mind that your feelings always follow your actions. Taking the proper actions will change your feelings. What actions are you taking to alter your emotional state?

According to the research by the Institute of Neuroscience and Psychology at the University of Glasgow the core emotions are:

Happiness: An emotional state of satisfaction.
Triggered Feelings: Joy, contentment, euphoria, deep satisfaction.

Sadness: An emotional state of hopelessness and disappointment.
Triggered Feelings: Disappointment, hopelessness, regret, grief.

Fear: This is a main emotional state key to human survival, it signals an internal alarm or warning.
Triggered Feelings: Aggression, defensiveness.

Anger: An emotional state of discontent capable of affecting the physical body.
Triggered Feelings: Frustration, enmity, aversion, aggression.

Surprise: Emotion reacting to something unexpected
Triggered Feeling: Crying, laughter, startled, shocked. These feelings may be positive or negative.

Disgust: An emotional state of strong repugnance.
Triggered Feeling: Sicken, disgust, dismay.
(University of West Alabama, 2019)

Things to ponder:

1. Can you identify an action you would implement that create the emotions you would like to experience and its corresponding feelings? (Make a list) This will help your awareness.

Notes:

_____

_____

_____

_____

_____

_____

_____

_____

_____

_____

_____

_____

_____

_____

_____

_____

_____

_____

_____

_____

_____

_____

_____

_____

_____

_____

Week Seven: Emotions

Day Two   *Date:*

Never let your emotions overpower your intelligence.

Responding or Reacting to Emotions?

Emotions have been shown to completely distort our ability to make sound decisions. Emotional decisions are focused on what you want or feel right now, not on what is best for you. To take control of your emotions, you need to make decisions with your head not with your heart, and if you are a believer you may want to seek God's guidance.

Determine if your emotions are positive or negative. Are you often falling into traps of emotional manipulation? Think of this, how you respond to your emotions will highly determine the outcome of your decisions. If you are a high "D" (Dominance) personality type, you may feel very comfortable making decisions. But, realistically speaking despite of the personality type, you can't just jump on a situation and make a decision out of thin air without first analyzing some type of information. What would your decision be based on? It can be based on data and information or plain emotions. Be careful with your emotions, they can be deceiving! Decisions made based on emotions often lead to regrets. Decisions rather should be based on careful meditation of data and facts, independent of how you feel or what type on personality type you have.

When you respond to your emotions you allow reason into the process; reacting, on the other hand, is an utter mindset chaos dominated by your emotional state of mind. No reason involved in the latter.

Things to Ponder:

1. Do you react? Or Do you Respond to your emotions?
2. Do emotions run your life? Or do you run your emotions?

Notes:

Week Seven: Emotions

Day Three   *Date:*

Feelings don't identify who you are.

DON'T Follow your Emotions!

Your brain is the most powerful machine ever created. Put it to work! You need to take control of your life, what you do, what you think, and what you feel. If you let your emotions go rampant, they will tear you apart. You must master your emotions and exercise discipline over them. You must be at the helm of your emotional state and have your emotions under your control. You must call the shots, otherwise you will remain shackled to your emotions and that is a very scary thought. You must discipline your emotions, or your emotions will discipline you. What is your choice?

Remember, emotions are your response mechanism triggered by actions and events. Therefore, if you learn how to control the way you react to events, your emotions will change. I am not implying for you to ignore your emotions. Rather exercise control over how they affect you and the outcome of your life especially if you tend to trigger negative feelings.

Pay attention to your responses or reactions, they may be reveling more than you care to admit.

Things to Ponder:

> *Exercise:* Make a list of the positive and negative emotions you need to deal with. List how do your emotions affect your day-to-day life?

Notes:

_____

_____

_____

_____

_____

_____

_____

_____

_____

_____

_____

_____

_____

_____

_____

_____

_____

_____

_____

_____

_____

_____

_____

_____

_____

Week Seven: Emotions

Day Four   *Date:*

If you don't discipline your emotions,

Emotions will discipline you.

Discipline Your Emotions!

This quote is so true. You may want to ask yourself, who is in charge? My emotions or myself? Therefore, putting your emotions under discipline will help you stay in control. Beware of how you respond or react to situations. Don't get distracted by your emotions, by procrastination, negative thoughts, irrelevant feelings, and events that will only get you sidetracked. Stay focused on what you need to do. Success is not about how you feel, it is about what you do. The right actions will trigger positive emotions. If you wait to feel good to "take action", you may never start!

- *Discipline will take you to the finish line*. A disciplined athlete will train no matter how good or bad he/she feels. An athlete trains because training will make them feel good despite the soreness and the pain the athlete may feel. Without a doubt, it will raise their spirits. Taking the right actions gives you a good feeling to know you are advancing towards your goals. It's the feeling of accomplishment that evokes good emotions, not the other way around.

Things to Ponder:

1. Do emotions get you into trouble?
2. Are your decisions driven by your emotions?
3. What are the things you know you should do but will not because your emotional state is often side tracking you?

Notes:

Week Seven: Emotions

The Power of Emotions

We experience both positive and negative emotions, and there is power in both. Positive emotions provide a level of pleasurable experience, and negative emotions provide a feeling of discontent. These emotions will create its own reaction and it's easier to respond to positive and pleasurable emotions than it is to emotions triggering a sense of discomfort.

Emotions can't be avoided, and neither can we allow emotions run unrestrained. Doing so, can cause much harm to our lives, relationships, and even our health. Emotions are meant to act as messengers, they deliver a message, they tell you something and if you pay attention it can work to your benefit.

For example, bursts of anger can be a sign of a deeper problem. To deal with anger requires reaching to the root of the emotion. You can't ignore your emotion and expect to heal and overcome, it requires addressing the issue. The healing process includes healing any root of anger before it turns into bitterness. Frustration, and resentment may also stem from deep roots worth looking into. We need to deal with the root causes. Listen, pay attention to your emotions, and how you respond or react to situations. They may be telling you more than meets the eye.

Be aware of your emotional state and connect with your emotions. Try to understand where they stem from. Be prompted to read your emotions because they carry an important message you need to decode. If your emotions are controlling your actions, it is time to take control. Be intentional, take over and keep them under control.

Things to Ponder:

1. What negative emotions trigger bad reactions in your life?
2. Meditate on what type of environment or situations trigger your negative emotions.

Notes:

_____

_____

_____

_____

_____

_____

_____

_____

_____

_____

_____

_____

_____

_____

_____

_____

_____

_____

_____

_____

_____

_____

_____

Week Seven: Emotions

Mastering Emotions

Emotions are a manifestation of energy, and energy is positive and negative. There are several strategies you can use to neutralize, or minimize the harm done by negative emotions. You must start by taking control of your emotions through change, and change starts with awareness.

One of my favorite strategies is the expression of gratitude. Expressing gratitude is a great way to neutralize bad vibes and negative energy. It has been shown that when we engage in daily gratitude exercises, our attitude, our feelings, and emotions shift from negative to positive. Affirm your heart with words of gratefulness. Also try ocean breathing exercises with a 4/4/4 breathing rhythm. You inhale deep for 4 seconds, hold your breath controlling your breath with your diaphragm for 4 sec. and breathe out through the nose for 4 sec. This exercise is calming and balancing for your mind as it helps you increase your awareness and concentration. It helps to reduce stress and tension, in addition to regulating body temperature. The benefits of beathing exercises are endless. It helps you exercise control over your negative emotions by changing your emotional state, from negative to positive, from sad to joy, from hopelessness to hopefulness, etc.

Remember, positive energy and emotions will bring about a greater sense of positiveness, optimism, and resilience towards the future. You have a better chance of success when you remain in control. Remain with your awareness switch ON. If you remain aware of when your negative emotions erupt, you are in a better position to stop; take deep breaths, and express words of affirmation to neutralize the negative thoughts. You can also reject any out of place negative comments, including your inner voice. Affirm yourself until you regain your balance. Remember, when you master your emotions, you remain in control.

Things to Ponder:

1. What emotions do you *not* control? (Think of an emotion that will ruin a moment or even a day; if it does, it controls you).
2. What situations or environment has trigged your reaction or response?

Notes:

_____

_____

_____

_____

_____

_____

_____

_____

_____

_____

_____

_____

_____

_____

_____

_____

_____

_____

_____

Week Seven: Emotions

Day Seven   *Date:*

Time to Reflect and Recharge, is time well spent!

Day of Reflection

It's been a few busy days, full of diagnosis and plans for transformational change. It's time to reflect on what you have learned so far. You can go to school, spend years reading inspiring self-improvement books, and that is great, but these are theoretical lessons. There is a significant difference between theory and practice, and a special magic in putting theory to work. I call it "applied knowledge". There is something special in the personal lessons learned along the way in our life. Lessons learned that lead to change. They are your own life lessons, lessons you can call your own.

These experiences are the making of who you are and the lessons that shape who you will become from this point forward. These are the lessons you will share with others as you share your life experiences and add-value to others around you. They are the making of your own personal story.

Things to Ponder:

1. What are your breakthroughs and take-aways for the past lessons?
2. What are the things you have learned about yourself that you had never thought about before?

Notes:

_____

_____

_____

_____

_____

_____

_____

Week Eight: Boundaries

Day One   *Date:*

The lack of Boundaries invites disrespect!

What are Boundaries?

When you want to go to a foreign country, chances are, you will need a visa or permit to allow your entry. That visa or permit has a purpose and a limit or duration of time. At entry, immigration will give you a clear and defined time limit of stay. Overstaying constitutes breaking the law and that, has consequences. The visitor will have to assume all responsibilities for abiding with the allowed time frame of stay. The host country visa also retains the right to revoke the visa at any time if the visitor for any reason does not respect the allotted time of stay. Now, think of yourself as a country with well-established borders. You choose when, how long and who is allowed inside your boundaries.

Same concept applies to your life and your relationships. When you do not set boundaries, people tend to overstay and violate your space. However, it is not entirely their fault if it is not clear what your boundaries are until you set them and enforce them. It is entirely your responsibility to have clear set and well-defined boundaries for people to abide by them.

Are you ready to establish limits in your life and make sure to enforce them?

Things to Ponder:

1. How often do you allow people to trespass and invade your territory?
2. Do you allow people to step into your private space, take more than you would like them to but are uneasy to say stop?
3. If so, do you have clear boundaries? If not, why not?

Notes:

_____

_____

_____

_____

_____

_____

_____

_____

_____

_____

_____

_____

_____

_____

_____

_____

_____

_____

_____

_____

_____

_____

_____

_____

_____

_____

_____

Laurina Emiliani

Week Eight: Boundaries

Day Two   Date:

No, is a complete sentence- Ann Lamott

Setting Boundaries

Setting boundaries is the key to establishing healthy relationships. For some people setting boundaries is a challenge. Often people fear confrontation, rejection, abandonment and even dealing with guilt for limiting others access to their territory and consequently, the prevailing emotion (fear) binds them to manipulation and abuse. The person with no set boundaries is giving up their right to protect their space and the environment that makes them feel comfortable, secure, and safe. This can happen in any relationship type, a friend, a teacher, a colleague, your children, spouse and even pets. You must be ready and willing to enforce your boundaries no matter the relationship.

If you are a people pleaser or if you live in co-dependent relationships, you may have a bigger problem. However, you can start by setting boundaries, learn to stand your ground by saying "no" without having to explain yourself. Know that you do not have to say "yes" when you really feel like saying "no". Keep in mind you are not responsible for anyone but yourself. Someone else's feelings or reactions are not your responsibility. Don't feel bound to provide something you are not responsible for. Once the concept of boundaries sinks in, you can be intentional in practicing it. The more you practice, the more comfortable you will feel with it, and the more comfortable you feel the easier it will be to enforce it.

Things to Ponder:

1. How comfortable do you feel saying "No"?
2. Do you allow people to invade your safe space, personally or professionally?
3. Are you subject to manipulation and abuse, if so by whom? (Identify the person)
4. What situations can you identify as manipulative or abusive in your life?

Notes:

_____

_____

_____

_____

_____

_____

_____

_____

_____

_____

_____

_____

_____

_____

_____

_____

_____

_____

Week Eight: Boundaries

Day Three   *Date:*

Break free by saying NO, without giving a reason!

Are you a People Pleaser?

Setting boundaries is important to live free and enjoy freedom. I struggled with this weakness until I understood I am not responsible to anyone but myself. It is not about being selfish, it's about setting boundaries. If you don't set boundaries, you expose yourself to abuse. Some people do not care to stop until you make them stop. The way to do that is by taking the stop sign out. Yes, the red stop signs in the street corner. People will continue taking from you until you set clear boundaries. You need to learn to say STOP and NO, while not feeling the need to explain yourself. When you do, you will know you have conquered this issue. It's important because it is a weakness hindering your growth and development, not only at a personal level, but also in business. You can keep your composure, be polite while still being firm. Stand your ground, it's your right!

Setting boundaries is extremely important. For example, sports delineate the court of play. When the ball goes out of bounds, the game stops. The ball is put back at play inside the court and the game continues. Again, countries have set boundaries. If someone wants to enter a country, the visitor must request a visa allowing entry otherwise access will be denied at the port of entry. Thus, boundaries are imaginary lines that define territories. The same concept applies to our lives, and the boundaries you set define your safe space. You choose who you connect with, who you allow in, how far in and how long. The boundaries you set must be respected by others without the fear of abrupt violation. Think that you manage your streetlights, you decide when you will have it in green, when people can freely advance. You decide when to exercise a "warning" and turn the light yellow, and finally you decide to turn the RED light on to make people STOP on their tracks.

From early childhood we should learn how to set boundaries and enforce them. The problem is that we are incapacitated by hostility, abuse, and inconsistent upbringing. Our upbringing will build bridges that help us connect with the world or will build walls that isolate us unable to connect with others in a healthy way. As such, people grow up unable to relate and connect with others and themselves. Most people are unable to recognize emotions, and feelings, therefore they grow up with indecisiveness for their lack of identity. We don't know who we really are and where we want to go. As a result, they don't know how to set boundaries, and some others don't know they can.

A healthy boundary is one that is well defined and easily identifiable. It is not a wall that keeps us isolated, rather it is a selective yet flexible boundary capable of protecting your safe space. Your boundaries are set not just by words but also kept and protected by your actions. It is your responsibility to make sure your boundaries are abided by, otherwise there is no point in having them altogether. We decide and we are responsible for keeping, guarding, and enforcing our boundaries. Animals do it, learn to establish and enforce them too.

Things to Ponder:

1. Do you have boundaries?
2. Are your boundaries clearly defined?
3. Can you say No, without feeling the urge to explain yourself?

Exercise:
Step 1: Make a list of people you have a hard time saying No to.
Step 2: Think of a time you said "Yes", when wanting to say "No", and later regretted it. Make note of the consequences.
Step 3: Define and delineate your boundaries. Set the things you should not allow in your life and be ready to say STOP or No, next time someone asks you to do anything you really don't want to do.
Step 4: Before you answer Yes, or No… think: "I am only responsible for myself!". You are not responsible for how other people feel or what other people do. If they get offended that is their choice, that is their problem. It's not yours to solve!
Step 5: Say No, without having to explain yourself.

Step 6: Be aware of your boundaries and promptly say STOP when you feel invaded. Red light 🚦 ahead!

Step 7: Be firm when defending your safe space. Remember, your safe space is not public space. It's your private space!

Notes:

_____

_____

_____

_____

_____

_____

_____

_____

_____

_____

_____

_____

_____

_____

_____

_____

_____

_____

_____

_____

_____

_____

Week Eight: Boundaries

Day Four   Date:

People are never able to outperform their self-image.

-John C Maxwell

Limiting Thoughts

If you don't believe you can, you probably won't. Our self-image and self-perception can be barriers in our lives. These barriers hinder your growth and progress. Barriers limit your potential creating an imaginary lid that will keep us trapped because we can never outgrow our self-image. John C Maxwell refers to this as the "Law of the Lid" in his book "The 15 Invaluable Laws of Growth." The value judgements we make upon ourselves will ultimately help us or hinder us. If you don't believe you are of any value, you don't have a chance of accomplishing goals and dreams. You need to feel you are capable before attempting to accomplish anything. Self-image is the perception you have of yourself, and that is a muscle helping you to push forward. If you think you can, then you will. It takes believing that you can, to ignite your will and get prepared to make it happen.

Self-esteem is a strong muscle pushing forward in your throttle. You must believe good things will happen, you need to believe, "I am capable", "I can do it", "I will do this", and say "I can do this, I will do this" as many times as it is necessary until you believe it!

Just as much as you internalized all the No's and the negative reinforcements you've heard and received since you were born and believed them; you also need to renew your mind in transforming those negatives into positives. Remember that *the value you give yourself, is the value others will see in you.* Many people live their lives based on what other people think of them basing their self-image in other people's opinions. They become dependent on someone else's opinion of them. *Don't be concerned with what people may think of you,* or if they believe you are capable or not. Remember, people don't throw stones at a tree that bears no fruit. Start by giving yourself daily words of affirmation, it will compound with time. One day, before you know it you will be feeling confident and giving someone else words of affirmation for a change.

Every evening before you go to bed and during the day read or listen to words of affirmations or bible promises. Take breaks during the day to have a one-minute self-talk to feed yourself words of affirmation in the areas you know are hindering your growth. As a result, you can then *take the lid off and rise to your potential!*

Things to Ponder:

1. Identify any limiting beliefs or mental barriers that you constantly battle with that prevent you from moving forward.

Notes:

_____

_____

_____

_____

_____

_____

_____

_____

_____

_____

_____

_____

_____

_____

_____

_____

_____

_____

Week Eight: Boundaries

Day Five   *Date:*

You are confined by the barriers you build around you!

Clear the Barriers

Success doesn't happen overnight and it's surely not accidental. To name just a few examples, we have Michael Jordan, Coby Bryant, Cristiano Ronaldo, and so many more top performers who have entertained us on the court and outside the court. We don't know how many hours were dedicated in training between games and before the rise to stardom. That we don't see, we only get to see their performance on the court. They train and they train hard. They also train their mind as much as they do their sport skills by destroying the decoys placed as mental barriers limiting growth. These barriers prevent people from rising to a higher level of performance in whatever they do. It is said that success is 80% attitude and 20 % skill. We spend a good portion of our time working on skills, which is the 20% of success, thus leaving attitude and mindset, the remaining 80%, totally unattended. It may seem hard to believe, but it is true. Our mindset will help us make it or break it. This journal is helping you work on that 80% we all need to master!

We encounter mental barriers all the time in different shapes and forms. Perception, toxic opinions, fear, and even bad news are real mental blockers that act as barriers hindering our effort to advance.

Yesterday you identified limiting thoughts and mental barriers that obstruct your path. Now, you need to engage in clearing these barriers from your lane. Clear up the road!

Things to Ponder:

Exercise: Carry the serenity prayer with you and use it as you encounter challenges in life. Know it by heart.

"God grant me the serenity to accept the things I cannot change; courage to change the things I can; and wisdom to know the difference."

Ways to Clear the Barriers:

1. Establish a routine for listening to words of affirmation to neutralize limiting thoughts before you go to sleep, or while resting and repeat them while you listen.
2. Steps to take may include removing toxic people from your life. This is often a very difficult decision; however, it may be the most liberating decision you'll make. You won't regret it.
   Can you identify toxic people and relationships you need to break from?
3. Stop giving so much credit to people's opinion (often is not even sincere or relevant).
4. Cast out fear, with a higher level of faith and courage. Do you struggle with fear? What type of fear do you struggle with the most?

Notes:

_____

_____

_____

_____

_____

_____

_____

_____

_____

_____

_____

_____

Week Eight: Boundaries

Day Six   Date:

To live is a value judgement, to breathe is to judge.

-Albert Camus

Value-Judgements

Value judgements are assessments made about events, experiences, or someone you relate to at any given moment. People don't realize they make value judgments all the time while making decisions, as they seek to determine what is important, what is of value to them, what they will pursue and what will be left behind.

Decisions are often based on our values and principles which gives our life structure. For the most part, value judgments precede decisions for better or worse. Decisions are made as you build or follow mental arguments you rely upon. Judgment skills are necessary in the decision-making process, no matter how simple or complex the situation may seem. Having the ability to make good judgement calls enables you to make effective decisions during critical situations. When we make accurate value judgments, we are likely to make sound decisions.

What you need to avoid is becoming an unmerciful critic of yourself and others. If you are to take a critical role, let it be for betterment, to add-value, to build and not to detonate destruction. Value judgements are positive actions when used as means for growth and learning, but if abused it can become very dark and negative. Make sure to be aware of the difference!

Things to Ponder:

1. What inflicting value judgements are you applying to yourself or others?
2. What areas in your life are you self-conscious and insecure about?
3. Are these areas worthy of change? And what steps are you willing to take to make changes possible?

Notes:

Week Eight: Boundaries

Day Seven   *Date:*

Setting Boundaries is having the courage to put ourselves first before everyone else, its self-respect!

Day of Reflection

S etting your foot forward takes courage and setting healthy boundaries is one of the most important steps towards your liberated life. You don't have to be bound by other's opinions and abuses. Implementing clear boundaries that people will easily respect is something you will need to practice. At first it may seem harsh, however be kind, caring but firm. No need to be pushy and impolite.

Take this time to meditate in the boundaries you need to set for yourself, and this applies to everyone, yes even your pet! Be honest, remember the truth shall set you free. Lack of boundaries always leads to disrespect. I don't know of anyone who enjoys being disrespected; so why should you? You do not have to deal with feeling disrespected any longer. Step up and don't allow any more disrespect, no matter who it is.

Things to Ponder:

1. Have you chosen the boundaries you need to set. Make a list.
2. How not establishing boundaries have affected your life and your performance? Think of ways you can establish boundaries in those areas, and clear mindset barriers that have kept you bound.
3. Remember to identify toxic people around you. Find ways to limit the time you spend with them. It will decrease your exposure to further abuse until you can cut them altogether.

Notes:

Week Nine: Decisions

Day One   *Date:*

The higher you climb, the tougher it is to let go!

Understanding Trade-Offs

Trade-offs are exchanges we make along our lives. In personal development, we must give-up some things that hinder our growth and exchange them for other more valuable things that will instead promote growth and development. Basically, we negotiate with ourselves as we constantly exchange one thing for another. When seeking change, we use trade-offs or exchanges as we move forward or else, we would be stuck in a place of discontent bearing no good fruit. The whole point is not to endure choices or just merely go through the process of making decisions without capitalizing on changes. The idea is learning through the process, because as you make choices you grow, and become a better person as a result.

Your choices and decisions will forcefully take you through changes in life, but all change is not for the better therefore, make sure trade-offs will provide positive results. Learn as you change and move forward in the growing and development process.

Avoid stepping on the same stone twice, making the same mistakes repeatedly, over, and over, and having the audacity to complain about making the same mistakes is not very wise. That is not growth, it is evidence of stagnation. Take responsibility for your actions. You will become a victim of your own negligent passiveness. In contrast, take control by becoming actively involved in making choices as you learn and grow during the process.

Sometimes people wait until the water is about to hit the ceiling to seek for help, thus change. You don't want to reach that point in your development. Heraclitus, a Greek philosopher, is quoted as saying "change is the only constant in life." Therefore, if change is a constant, we never cease to change. The key is, are you learning and applying what you learn or are you merely enduring the process? Only when you learn, you develop and grow. In this process, you must learn the art of trade-off. This exchange is at the core of change, and you must appreciate it and recognize it as part of the process.

You must be ready, willing, and able to exercise change by accepting trade-offs. You trade off one thing for something better. Sometimes people reject change for the fear of something new. They don't feel comfortable walking outside their comfort zone. Accepting change takes courage and a bold attitude to explore and commit to follow through. Without change, there is no progress!

Things to Ponder:

1. In what area of your life are you repeatedly falling in the same pothole without learning, without gain or experiencing growth? (Make a list)
2. Is there a lesson to learn now that would avoid you from falling into the same trap again? What can you do differently to successfully implement change.

Notes:

_____

_____

_____

_____

_____

_____

_____

_____

_____

_____

_____

Week Nine: Decisions

To decide is to assume the consequences.

Decision Making

There are two types of decision making, active and passive. Active decision making is the process by which reflection or analysis of information is used to evaluate and consider, options and alternatives available to us. The intention behind decision-making is to resolve problems or eliminate barriers. An active decision maker *responds* rather than react to situations. The whole point of moving forward in problem resolution is to relieve tension, therefore the process should not add to the stress. On the contrary, resolving problems should serve to relieve stress.

Passive decision making, on the other hand, is favoring the easy way-out option. No information is requested, no information is sought out, just the easiest most convenient decision now. It may or may not be the best option. The point in passive decision making is to get rid of the issue and move on despite of consequences. Understandably so, being a passive decision maker may not provide the best or more desirable outcome. When making decisions, your position should be to look for the best alternative as you reach for the best possible outcome.

As you ponder on how emotions affect your decision making and how it affects your life, think about, and reflect on what you have learned during the past weeks and what you can do to be more aware of your decision-making strategies. You can become an active decision maker and be more effective in problem resolution processes by adapting certain habits nesting "call to action", triggering a response rather than a "reaction". Remember, decisions made based on emotions most always end up in regret. A passive decision-making strategy does not aim to resolve a problem, rather to move it away.

Identify your decision-making strategy and move forward to take the proper actions to avoid regret in the future. Become an active decision maker by becoming aware of the strategy when making decisions.

Things to Ponder:

1. Do you consider yourself an Active or a Passive decision-maker?
2. If passive, are you willing to work on strategies to change from passive to Active? If so, how are you planning on implementing change?

Notes:

_____

_____

_____

_____

_____

_____

_____

_____

_____

_____

_____

_____

_____

_____

_____

_____

_____

_____

Week Nine: Decisions

Day Three   *Date:*

My choices today, will shape my tomorrow!

Decision Making Strategies

If you are a passive decision maker, you need to flip the switch to change. Shift your gear from a passive to an active decision making. Taking the proper steps to arrive to a sound decision, one that will edify your life and improve a situation or whatever problem you are resolving is key for your overall effectiveness and performance throughout your life. Proper evaluation of gathered information is essential to anyone in business, family, relationship, or professional career.

Everything starts by adopting a good strategy that will help you grow and improve your decision-making skills. These strategies become habits that are formed when the right strategies are applied consistently every time you are confronted with a decision. It is important to know good decisions most often stem from the analysis of data and information available about a situation. This is why it's important to adopt an action-based strategy using the analysis of data and information, rather than a reaction-based strategy founded solely on emotions. If you don't want to live with regret, avoid it!

Below find the steps required for an *action-based decision-making* strategy:

1. Know your goals (What do you want to accomplish? And stay focused)
2. Gather data and information (This will help you make an informed decision)
3. Stay open-minded (Don't be stuck, there is always room for improvement)
4. Review all your options and scenarios.
5. Consider the consequences for each option (Write a list of Pro's and Con's)
6. Based on the list, eliminate bad options (Which option provides the best value to your goal?)
7. Prepare to confront and mitigate consequences.
8. Be responsible and own it. If you want to learn and grow, be ready to take the credit or to admit you were wrong as a result.

Things to Ponder:

1. Are you willing to adopt the above action-based strategy to decision making? You must STOP, when pressured to decide. If you doubt, the decision should be No. (keep and protect your boundaries)
2. If you are willing, make an exact list as above and save it on your phone notes. Have it available for you to follow each point and allow it to lead you to becoming an *Action-Based* decision maker. Practice it!

Notes:

_____

_____

_____

_____

_____

_____

_____

_____

_____

_____

_____

_____

_____

_____

_____

_____

_____

_____

_____

Week Nine: Decisions

Day Four   *Date:*

Bad habits hinder, good habits enable!

My Habits

Habits are behaviors our brain has on autopilot. It stems from doing something repeatedly until it becomes embedded in our brain. We do this throughout our lives without even realizing it. That is how we end up with common habits, some promoting growth and others simply hinder our development. We don't need to think about it, it just happens. It's like muscle memory, like keyboard shortcuts for our brain.

Let's start by identifying good habits to affirm and bad habits to replace. This will lead you to transform your daily routines and should provide a healthier, more productive, and effective lifestyle. Bad habits can impact your life negatively by hindering your progress, damaging your health and well-being, ultimately affecting your mood, and robbing you of the joy of life.

Figuring out your bad habits is a good place to start. Meditate on which habits originate bad emotions and which situations trigger your bad habits. (Refresh your memory by going back to review the week you pondered on emotions). Repeating the action enough times is sufficient to create a habit. It is said it takes 21 days to adopt a habit. These continuous repetitive actions are the "Save" button that turn actions into habits. Some habits are triggered by negative emotions, and they are not exempt of consequences in your life. It is important to be aware of any negative emotions and the habits they help us create.

Diagnosing your bad habits will not only help you develop awareness in your behavior but will also help you find alternative routines triggering positive results and outcomes. Therefore, you need to work to replace bad habits with good, positive habits that edify your life. Consider that good emotions will follow positive actions leading to adopting good habits we all should have.

The goal is for you to replace bad habits with good habits helping you move forward. Go back to week seven and review what you wrote about emotions. Which are the emotions you listed as good and positive emotions? Consider which habits will they inhibit, and which will trigger positive emotions. Remember, emotions will follow the right action. Adopt habits with the "right actions" required to move on the positive direction.

Things to Ponder:

1. What are the habits you recognize in your life?
2. Which ones are positive, and which ones are negative?
>   (Make a list and its consequences)

Notes:

_____

_____

_____

_____

_____

_____

_____

_____

_____

_____

_____

_____

_____

_____

_____

Laurina Emiliani

Week Nine: Decisions

Day Five   *Date:*

You must give up, to grow up! -John C Maxwell

Decoding Bad Habits

Now that you have identified bad habits in your life, it's time to decide which habits you need to change for your own good, betterment, and growth. The voyage of transformation includes the "changing your bad habits tour" and become all that you were meant to be. Let's start by dissecting a habit…

There are 3 main components of a habit:

1. *Trigger:* The action or situation that leads to an emotional reaction.
2. *Habit:* An involuntary manner of behavior
3. *Reward:* Something received as recognition or achievement for an effort.

Steps to Change Habits:

Step 1
Diagnosis: To change a habit, you need to identify it.

Step 2
Changes: Change the environment that triggers or nourishes the habit. You need to starve it!

For example, if you are used to munching junk food while watching TV when you get home from work or school, instead of fighting the habit, just start by stopping the trigger. The trigger is the action that leads to the habit. In this case, choose not to watch TV (the trigger). Thus, choose to replace the behavior, go for a walk instead. Maybe you can find a better activity, go to the gym, or perhaps take a stroll at the local park, it may create the good habit of exercising instead of being a "couch potato". The gym or an afternoon stroll will replace the bad habit you have created with a good habit if you consistently practice it. If you enjoy reading, this may be a good time to pick up a book instead. You need to remember to keep your routine for a while until it becomes part of you. You will feel a void when you get out of your routine.

For each bad habit identified, try to think of a positive behavior you can replace your bad habit with and break the bad habit to replace it with a positive behavior. Make a list and choose to change one habit at a time. Remember, it is repeated actions that create habits. Remember, being brutally honest is key. There is no sense in hiding the facts. It will only hurt yourself.

Step 3:

Reward: Don't lose focus of the reward. The reward is what fills your inner needs. For example, addictions are habits, and they falsely fulfill an inner need. It gives you a numbing sensation, but the pain will not go away. Maybe it's a substance or a behavioral addiction you want to break. If it takes 21 days to create a habit, how long will it take for you to break it? Take one bad habit a time. Imagine breaking a bad habit every month until you beat them all. How would your life be transformed at the end of one year?

If it doesn't edify, it destroys! At the end of the day, it is your decision. The point is not to continue numbing your pain, rather as a better alternative, consider healing the cause or root of the pain. Remember, if the roots of a tree are not healthy, the tree will not bear good fruit. Heal the roots and your fruit shall be sweet and healthy. Make the decision to replace bad habits and allow yourself to grow into a better you. You must confront the pain to heal. You heal by coming to terms with the truth. The truth shall set you free!

Things to Ponder:

1. Make a list of your good and bad habits.
2. Which habits of the list hurt your chances of growth the most, and how?

Good Habits   *Bad Habits*

_____   _____

_____   _____

_____   _____

_____   _____

_____   _____

_____   _____

_____   _____

_____   _____

_____   _____

_____   _____

_____   _____

_____   _____

_____   _____

_____   _____

Notes:

Week Nine: Decisions

Day Six   *Date:*

A habit is unnoticeable until its burden is too heavy to be broken.

Breaking the Habit!

Breaking a habit is an individual experience. For someone with a high level of determination will take less time than for someone with a low level of determination. Some deep-rooted habits may take as long as a year of grappling with the weakness. The timeframe to break out of a habit will differ, but to conquer it will take identifying the trigger, setting realistic goals, be absolutely convinced of the purpose, and having an absolute determination. These steps will help you break free from the bondage of a bad habit.

Your mindset is key in beating any bad habit you will confront. Follow the steps provided on day five and be absolutely determined to change. Change is essential to breaking habits, unless you want to continue in the path you were headed. However, if you are not happy with your life's path, the only hope is implementing change. It is you and only you who will determine the path you will take. You can't blame anyone for the path you have chosen. You must take responsibility for the route you have given your life. Your habits will determine your future.

Habits are very hard to eradicate. Therefore, seek to change the environment and the trigger for the habits you are trying to get rid of. Otherwise, you will repeatedly fall victim to falling back to the unfortunate situation, no matter how many times you try. The routine you adopt is the link to the reward, and it must be changed.

To truly break a habit, you need to change the environment and replace it with a better, more edifying path. Choose something that you and those around you would enjoy, something that will bring a sense of fulfillment. This will make it easier and attainable.

Things to Ponder:

1. What actions do you need to implement for you to effectuate the changes required to eradicate bad habits?

Notes:

_____

_____

_____

_____

_____

_____

_____

_____

_____

_____

_____

_____

_____

_____

_____

_____

_____

_____

_____

_____

_____

_____

_____

_____

Week Nine: Decisions

Day Seven   *Date:*
Reflection time allows us to reenergize.

Day of Reflection

Taking time to reflect is an important way to recharge energy and pick up your pace to move forward. Sometimes we are very busy pushing forward and we lose track of our path disregarding where we are. It is important to slow down to review the action plan to see ways you can tweak it and improve your position.

Don't think a quick stop to reflect will slow you down, because it may be the biggest push forward you get in your journey. Taking time to reflect will help you regain the energy you need to push forward and gain momentum. Once you have a clear picture of the plan, you will be better positioned to regain momentum. Once you regain momentum you can move with full force forward.

Things to Ponder:

1. What changes have you committed to that you have not implemented?
2. Has the inability to implement, hindered your growth and development?

Notes:

_____

_____

_____

_____

_____

_____

_____

Week Ten: Do you have what it takes?

Day One   *Date:*

The meaning of life is to find your gift,
the purpose of life is to give it away- William Shakespeare

My Gifts and Talents

We don't get to choose our gifts and talents. It's not like we send God a list of our wants, and musts, and they are provided. We get what we get, and it goes according to our calling. God purposedly gifted you, it is not a random act. Thus, we need to be good stewards of our God's given gifts and talents and put them to productive use. We all should want to make sure we capitalize on them. So how do we do that? The first step to change is always diagnosis. Therefore, recognizing your gifts and talents and manifesting graceful gratitude for them is a good start. Doing this every day and every night before you go to bed is a good way to renew your mind and reassure your heart.

Usually, the things you most enjoy are part of your gifts and talents. You must be willing to get out of your comfort zone and take risks to develop them. Take the steps to keep your gifts alive and growing! The whole purpose behind gifts, talents, skills, and knowledge and a way to give back is to put them to productive use. You can never fulfill your purpose if you don't use your resources. You can't live a fulfilled life if you hide your talents in a treasure box and leave them unused to waste. You need to use them, wear them like you would a new garment you'd love to show off. The garment would be of no-good use if it's hung in your closet and its never used. It will only build dust. Take charge, dust-off your gifts and talents and put them to good productive use!

Let's start by identifying your gifts and talents.... Are you ready?

157

Things to Ponder:

1. What would you like to do?
2. If you had to describe your dream job or business, how would it be?
3. What do you enjoy doing?

Notes:

_____

_____

_____

_____

_____

_____

_____

_____

_____

_____

_____

_____

_____

_____

_____

_____

_____

_____

_____

_____

_____

_____

_____

_____

Week Ten: Do you have what it takes?

Day Two   Date

Life is not a dress rehearsal- Peanuts

What do you enjoy doing?

I ask you what you like doing because you should do what you enjoy. How many people are stuck in a career, a job, or a business they hate? They are stuck at work, unmotivated not reaching their utmost potential because they lack passion. But if you do something you like and have a passion for it, you will never work a day in your life! What you like to do will lead you to your passion and your passion will uncover who you want to become.

We live once, and life is not a dress rehearsal. Think of your life as the Olympics games and you are going for the gold. You get one shot at winning. There is no doing it over. That comes before the competition. It is all a matter of timing your entry. You should strategize your life just as if you were one of the Olympic game's participants. If you are a believer, you may pursue the guidance of God, or perhaps a good coach or mentor. Whichever way you choose, you should **pursue your purpose with passion**.

Pay close attention to the extracurricular activities you enjoy, or the way you prefer to spend your free time. For example, if you enjoy reading, research, or learning, you may have a passion for activities that involve writing, educating, and training. Therefore, you should look for ways to solve a problem in areas that may result in a high demand activity you may like to pursue as a business, a side-hustle, or a civic cause. If you enjoy fixing things or putting things together, you may be a person with high level creativity. Think of ways you can put your creativity to work. If being on the move, exercising, dancing, bicycling or sports in general is your thing, then you may enjoy activities that involve corporal expression. Activities that involve diverse forms of expression include public speaking, communications, or not-for-profit work. There is a vast variety of activities and careers to pursue.

You must make sure you choose well because spending most of your day performing unfulfilling activities is wasting your life in a field you don't enjoy. It can lead to frustration and an unfulfilled life full of discouragement.

This is one thing you need to give a good deal of thought. Make sure you make the right choice. You may need to provide yourself with a list of choices. Do the proper analysis. Be an active thinker.

Things to Ponder:

Review the gift and talents journal lesson you completed and review the following:

1. What are you good at? In what activities are you above average?

   If you are good at something, it often falls within your gifts and talents or your strengths. If it does, then it qualifies as a profession or a business. If you are NOT good at it, and you enjoy it… it looks like it would be a great hobby you would like to practice for fun. Enjoying something is not enough, you must excel at it to rise above the average. You can't focus on a weakness and succeed. However, if instead, you focus on activities within your strengths and delegate on your weakness, it will take you further, much faster.

Notes:

_____

_____

_____

_____

_____

_____

_____

_____

_____

_____

_____

_____

Week Ten: Do you have what it takes?

Day Three   Date:

Genius is where creativity meets patience.

Aptitude and Skills

Aptitude is defined as the natural ability to do something. In other words, your capabilities. There is a special talent embedded within you to perform or produce certain things. If what you do falls withing your talents and gifts, and you excel at it, you should perform at above average standards. It is as important to know what you enjoy doing, as it is recognizing if you are any good at what you do. If you are not above average, then it looks like it falls in the hobby bucket rather than in the career or business bucket. You must be good at what you do to be outstanding at whatever you do.

It is important to recognize that to reach excellence, you should not work from your weakness; you should work from your strengths. Focus on your strengths and delegate tasks that fall within your weaknesses. Learn to team up with people who will complement you. The basis of teamwork is the ability to complement each other for the best of the team. You have heard, there is no "i" in team. Learning the value in delegating tasks that don't fall within your strengths is a huge step in reaching success. When you delegate tasks that fall within your weakness and focus to work within your strengths then you will find yourself rising to above average standards and as a result you can be outstanding.

Things to Ponder:

1. Think of activities you enjoy doing, can you identify a need in the market you could resolve?
2. Which activities can become opportunities you can capitalize on?

Notes:

_____

_____

_____

_____

_____

_____

_____

_____

_____

_____

_____

_____

_____

_____

_____

_____

_____

_____

_____

_____

_____

_____

_____

_____

Week Ten: Do you have what it takes?

Day Four   *Date:*

Show me your friends, and I will tell you who you are!

-Unknown

Who is my Inner Circle?

The environment where you live will shape your life in more ways than we care to admit. We are social beings seeking for connection. We have a profound need to connect and as a result, we engage in relationships. Culture is a powerful environment that greatly influences how you behave and how you engage with others. From childhood you start interacting with people and that engagement is the make-up of the social reality that will shape the way you relate with others as adults.

If you surround yourself with people playing victim mentality, you will be dragged into a victim state of mind. If you hang out with drug addicts, you will be dragged into addictions. If your inner circle sucks at keeping relationships, soon enough you will suck at relationships too. Their habits will soon become your habits. As relational beings, we tend to be influenced by relationship dynamics the most. We absorb what's in our environment. We are like sponges and our environment is what we absorb. We need to recognize that we are the average of the five people who most closely surround us. As the adage says, "how can I soar like an eagle, when I'm working with turkeys." Turkeys do not soar in flight. Thus, if what you want is to fly high and soar in flight, then hanging around with turkeys will not cut it for you. In that case you need a flock of eagles to hang out with. Your environment is your most severe source of influence.

On the other hand, if you surround yourself with high achievers, you will duplicate the high achieving habits and finally become a high achiever as well. As a result, you need to pay close attention to whom you choose to spend your time with, whether at work or socially. The more you spend time with, the deeper the roots of influence. If you must choose people to form teams, choose the ones you have the most chances of achieving goals, not those who will bring you down, no matter how "cool" they may appear.

The environment you choose will determine your future and your reaching success. Your environment can be a steppingstone to success, or a trap into failure.

Things to Ponder:

1. Who is in your inner circle?
2. Is your inner circle taking you to accomplish your goals?
3. Who can you keep in your inner circle and who do you need to let go to get where I want to go?

Notes:

_____

_____

_____

_____

_____

_____

_____

_____

_____

_____

_____

_____

_____

_____

_____

_____

_____

_____

_____

Week Ten: Do you have what it takes?

Day Five   Date:

If I don't control my environment, my environment will absorb me.

Environment or Genetics, which is a stronger influence?

Epigenetics is an emerging area of scientific research showing how the environment shapes a person's life and how it affects the expression of genes. In other words, its theory is centered in disproving the idea that genes can't be influenced. Our environment and life experiences directly reflect on our mind and body. I am in no way diminishing the role of genetics in our lives, however with this discovery we can understand the power our environment has and how it can influence our lives. The influence of genetics is more than a tendency, whereas the environment provides direction to individuals. By changing our environment, we can change the outcome of illnesses, such as depression. People may have the tendency for depression, and the environment they move in may signal its direction; however, in this case, the environment may give depression a green light to move forward or a red light to stop. Therefore, pay attention to whom you surround yourself with. It may determine the direction of your life.

Be choosy and picky on who you let into your inner circle because our genes are influenced by external stimuli. For example, stress is a strong component of external stimulus and the consequences it has in our minds and bodies can't be ignored. Stress causes inflammation, and it has consequences that may branch out into certain illnesses affecting us, if we are overly exposed to it. So, take care of the environment you create for yourself. Your friends, the people at work, and how we handle work pressures are part of your external stimulus. Everyone and everything that surrounds you will influence your moving forward, your growth and ultimately the outcome of your life.

Things to Ponder:

1. What type of environment do you live in?
2. What changes do you need to implement to improve your environment?
3. What type of environment do you think will improve the quality of your life?

Notes:

_____

_____

_____

_____

_____

_____

_____

_____

_____

_____

_____

_____

_____

_____

_____

_____

_____

_____

_____

_____

_____

_____

_____

Week Ten: Do you have what it takes?

Day Six   Date:

Small changes compound with time!

My Call-to-Action

S o far, you have meditated on decisions, habits, and how experiences forge changes in your life. You have also reflected on how these experiences prune you and how you can take control by "taking action" in the process of change. You can't allow yourself to fall prey to a victim mentality, consequently sending you in a down spiral of failures and bad decisions. Rather, you must set yourself to take control of what you feed your brain and your heart. You must learn the art of the trade-offs because you need to exercise the power of "choice" and take responsibility for the choices you make. As you live in awareness, only through insightful exchange of trade-offs, you can reach your utmost potential. Always be aware of your choices and the consequences these choices will bring to your life. If it is your choice, it is also your responsibility. Own it!

Things to Ponder:

1. How can you apply what you have learned so far to improve the condition of your life?
2. Name an accountability partner that will hold you accountable for the commitments you are making with this journal. Speak with this person and have them commit to helping you with the accountability process.

Notes:

Week Ten: Do you have what it takes?

Day of Reflection

In discovering your purpose, you must become aware of who you are, and what you are passionate for, because *when you discover your passion, you find your purpose.* It takes time to reflect and ask yourself questions leading you to finding your passion. To stimulate creativity and critical thinking, your questions must be focused on what you are trying to accomplish. The way people approach life lessons will determine if they will be winners or losers. *It takes questioning to extract the answers you need and fulfill what you expect.*

Things to Ponder:

1. What do you do that can easily make you lose track of time?
2. What makes you light up so much, you can talk about for hours without noticing?
3. Name 3 things you would like to be remembered for?
4. If you had no need to work, what would you choose to do?

5. What do you feel as fulfilling, enjoyable and of substance?
6. What do you find draining and stressful in your life?
7. Describe your ideal job or activity?

Notes:

_____

_____

_____

_____

_____

Laurina Emiliani

Week Eleven: Making it Happen!

Day One   *Date:*

Passion is the fire that lights up your motivation!

Discovering your Passion

Passion is a strong desire, a fire that lights up your motivation to push forward. Passion inspires, it moves your most inner desires to create and develop new ideas. It is an impulse, a spontaneous inclination or devotion to certain activities, concepts, or fields of study.

When you have passion, you tend to be resilient to beat the odds and push forward despite the obstacles you may encounter along the way. When you find your passion, you love what you do and when you do what you love, you will never "work" a day in your life. It is not so much about the money, money is a welcomed reward, but it should not be your core motivator. Rather, money is the result or the reward of the enjoyable effort.

Passion generates positive emotions. It will make you feel alive, excited, driven and perhaps euphorically energized towards reaching goals and accomplishments. Be mindful of your passion if you want to live your purpose. Passion and purpose are closely linked. Passion without purpose lacks direction, and it will remain an unaimed emotion with no fulfillment. Passion is an emotion; it is the energy that feeds an innate interest. Our purpose, on the other hand, has the conviction to fulfill your "why". Passion is not more important than purpose, rather passion will lead you into fulfilling your purpose when you discover your why.

Get ready to discover your passion!

Things to Ponder:

1. What is your passion?

Notes:

_____

_____

_____

_____

_____

_____

_____

_____

_____

_____

_____

_____

_____

_____

_____

_____

_____

_____

_____

_____

_____

My Passion:

_____

_____

_____

_____

Week Eleven: Making it Happen!

Day One   Date

Your achievements are the things you do,

your passion is who you are.

From Passion to Calling

The Cambridge English Dictionary defines passion as "an extreme interest or wish for doing something." So, in essence passion is an emotion tied to a strong interest you have for something you want to accomplish. This is a force or electrical charge that impulses you to overcome obstacles and finally accomplish a goal or a set of previously established goals. Passion goes hand in hand with motivation. Think of life as a combustion-engine converting energy from the heat of burning fuel into mechanical work or torque.

Passion is the energy required in your life to turn on the spark of motivation and get you started. Discipline, on the other hand, is the mechanical movements, the torque, that puts the engine on the move. It keeps you going! You need to be passionate about what you do, to keep you motivated and disciplined to make it happen. Remember to refuel your life (engine) and keep the spark of passion and motivation alive without giving up despite of difficulties!

To keep your passion on fire you must first discover it. To discover your passion, you need to not care about other's expectations and what other people think or expect of you. Focus on what you expect of yourself. Passion is not cognitive, rather its stems from the heart. You must discover your passion and what you have been awarded with. You touched on self-awareness at the beginning of the journal. This would be a good time to revisit what you wrote back then and see how much your self-awareness has evolved since then. You need to know yourself and dig deep in your heart to discover your passion. Your passion may be lying somewhere inside your heart totally undiscovered.

Or you may already know it but have not made a connection with it yet. It is dormant, ready to be awakened.

Your achievements are the things you do, they should reflect on your passion, and who you are. Your work and your passion should be perfectly aligned. So, let's discover your true passion and let your fire shine.

Things to ponder:

1. If I ask you to speak about something for 30 minutes without prepping time, what would you choose to speak about?

Notes:

_____

_____

_____

_____

_____

_____

_____

_____

_____

_____

_____

_____

_____

_____

_____

_____

_____

_____

Week Eleven: Making it Happen!

Day Three   Date:

If you know your purpose, you will fulfil your calling!

Your Life's Purpose and Calling

What is life without a purpose? An unfulfilled life is a very empty place lacking substance. *Your purpose is your destination, and the calling is the how you'll get there. Your purpose is what are you here on earth to accomplish* and *your calling is how you will accomplish your life's purpose.* I hope you see and understand how essential and important it is to make sure to accomplish the mission we have been delegated from above and our responsibility to accomplish it. First and foremost, you need to make sure to identify both.

There are four key points in discovering your purpose and fulfilling your calling:

1) *Self-Awareness*   3) *Attitude*
2) *Gratitude*   4) *Time of Reflection*

Firstly, self-awareness puts you in touch with yourself, and the more intense the intimacy the more in-touch you'll be with your surroundings. You must know yourself enough to truly create the type of awareness that impacts your daily life. When you are in touch with yourself, its easier to get connected with God. Your awareness allows the connection in the stillness of your mind and your spirit.

Find time to be alone and learn to enjoy your alone time. Put time aside to be idle and not be on the move. You don't have to be on the go all the time, always moving and doing something. It is good to rest and enjoy yourself and the environment you create for this special alone time. Use this time for meditation, to listen to God's instructions. You may also do something you enjoy like listening to or play music, a stroll in the park, or at the beach, or maybe cook a special meal for yourself. If you enjoy reading, grab a good book or a magazine you like. Take a good relaxing aromatherapy bath or watch a good movie, at home or at the cinema.

People say it's weird to go to the movies alone. At the end of the day, you are not there for a good conversation, you are there to watch a movie and that's exactly what you are doing at the movies being alone or with company. So, what is the deal about going by yourself to enjoy a movie at the cinema? Nonsense!

The point is to pamper yourself by yourself and while you are at it, become aware of your likes, and dislikes. The things you truly enjoy are the things that give you a sense of relaxation, which often, generate positive emotions. The dislikes generate negative emotions, those things that stress you out. Become aware of who you are deep inside and stay connected with yourself. Do things that create positive emotions, keep the likes, and push the dislikes away.

Do not fear of making the changes you need to grow. You will thank yourself when you do!

Things to Ponder:

1. Meditate on your journaling. One of the best ways to improve self-awareness is through journaling. It helps you learn about yourself and keeps you connected.

Notes:

_____

_____

_____

_____

_____

_____

_____

Week Eleven: Making it Happen!

Day Four   *Date:*

Gratitude is the purest expression of love!

Gratitude

The second point in discovering and fulfilling your purpose is *gratitude*. Most parents make sure to teach children to say please and thank you from early childhood. It is a social rule of good manners taught from early years. But one thing is saying thank you and another is being grateful. Gratefulness is so much deeper than just a social rule of good manners. It is more than a mere emotion; it is a condition of the heart. It is a conscious effort, a way of life.

A grateful heart sees things from a different perspective. A grateful heart thinks that no matter how bad things look, you know it will work out for the best. Often people tend to spend more time thinking about bad things, instead of expressing gratitude for the good things they experience, for what they do have, and the blessings received. Sometimes even something that now is apparently bad, turns out to be a blessing at the end. Don't let your "Thank you" be just mere words without meaning. Say what you mean and mean what you say. Give some substance to your "Thank you". Own it and mean it!

Psychology has performed much research about the impact gratefulness has in our lives and health. Evidence shows that those who practice gratefulness, those who count their blessings, those who choose to look at the glass half full rather than half empty live more fulfilled, happy, and healthy lives. Thus, adopting a lifestyle of gratefulness will help you become more fulfilled, happier, and less prone to depression and living with negative thoughts.

Start your day by expressing gratitude for every blessing you have and will receive. The attitude of your heart will reflect on everything you do. Selfishness will take you nowhere good. It is a lonely place of emptiness that provides no fulfillment. Work on your heart and your attitude towards life and your environment. You are in this world to serve, not to be served. When you give you receive, it is an unbreakable law of nature. You must sow to harvest. Flip the switch to a better you by making gratefulness a pilar in your life, a standard by which you live. Quit any attitude of complaint and allow gratitude flow from your heart to see your life flourish.

Things to Ponder:

Exercise your gratefulness muscle: From now on, every night before going to bed, take your journal and write three things that went well today that you can be grateful for. (Adopt this daily discipline, not just at the Thanksgiving holiday!)

Today I am grateful for:

1. _____
   _____
   _____
   _____

2. _____
   _____
   _____
   _____

3. _____
   _____
   _____
   _____

Week Eleven: Making it Happen!

Day Five   *Date:*

My attitude will determine my altitude! -Unknown

Attitude

The third point in discovering and fulfilling your purpose is *attitude*. We are pressed daily to perform in every level of our lives. There is pressure from every corner demanding high level performance. Life rewards the winners, and losers are set aside. The question is, how do we make sure to stand on the winning side and avoid losing? We can't win all the time, but we can approach life with a positive attitude and a winning mentality. That will make all the difference in the world.

It is evident discouragement can tamper our positiveness. It is ok to feel bummed out every now and then, but we can't allow discouragement to take us out of the game. When we fall, we need to shake the dirt off, get back up and get to work! How we approach problems, struggles and disappointments will determine the outcome of any endeavor.

You should be cautious of certain emotions and feelings that could potentially damage your attitude. The following could raise red flags in your life:

1. *Rejection can cripple your self-image if you allow it.*
2. *Resentment is a source of bitterness. Forgive, set yourself free, and move on!*
3. *Negativity is a recipe for failures. Negative energy neutralizes the positive.*

You must always pursue ways to improve and keep your winning attitude alive. You must never allow your positive attitude to dwindle, it's a goal you must accomplish daily.

These are daily habits to help you:

- *Journal every day, or as often as you can.*
- *Keep smiling!*
- *Wish people well.*
- *Be grateful (remember the daily gratefulness exercise: 3 things you can be grateful for every day)*
- *Practice a NO gossip policy.*
- *Stay optimistic.*
- *Listen to uplifting music (Positive message)*
- *Choose your inner circle carefully.*

Things to Ponder:

1. Is my attitude positive or negative?

Notes:

_____

_____

_____

_____

_____

_____

_____

_____

_____

_____

_____

_____

_____

_____

Laurina Emiliani

Week Eleven: Making It Happen!

Day Six   Date:

When you understand your purpose,

you find a way to make it happen!

Exercising your Calling

Most people have a sincere desire to fulfill their purpose in life. You need to carefully reflect on both your purpose and calling because there is a clear difference many people miss to identify. To fulfill your purpose, aim at ways to serve others rather than be served. Fulfilling your purpose will give you a sense of greater satisfaction and joy as you aim to reach fulfillment. No money in the world will give you the gratification you get when you live within your calling, as you pursue your purpose. Purpose is your assignment given to you by God. Why are you here on earth? Our purpose is to glorify God in all we do, to serve others, and to be productive members of society. That is our assignment.

Our calling is unique for each of us, and most of us have an inner desire to fulfill it. As relational beings your calling stems from engaging with others and using your gifts and talents as means to connect. Unfortunately, many end up drifting through life with no lighthouse in sight. Our calling is not making money or going to college. These are goals we want to accomplish, and they stem from preconceived ideas of what is required to succeed. Unfortunately, these achievements not always lead to fulfilling our calling. *Our calling is **how** you will fulfil your purpose, how you will make a difference in society*, or how you create something of significance to impact the people around you or in the world. Your calling is about how to make a difference the world we live in, to our neighborhoods, family, friends, or even your workplace. Your calling is your footprint, your legacy. It will identify you forever!

Often the root of pain may provide a path to fulfilling your calling. Looking at problems and challenges as an opportunity to grow and expressing

185

gratefulness are two main pillars in living a fulfilled life. Having clarity in your calling will provide direction to places and experiences enhancing and enlightening your soul. Experiences may very well turn into a waving flag calling for your attention. For this reason, keep your awareness lit up! You don't want to miss important messages life is sending you.

Meditate on your vision and your passion. They should lead you into ways of making a difference in identifying and fulfilling your calling. Start small and dream big!

Tips to fulfilling your calling:

- Persevere despite the challenges
- Embrace change
- Look at challenges not as problems, but as opportunities
- Be clear on your vision and don't lose sight of your purpose. (What do you want to accomplish in 10 years)

Things to Ponder:

1. What do you identify as your calling? Write it for your record on next page.
2. What can you do to work on your calling?
3. What changes can you implement to make it happen?

Notes:

_____

_____

_____

_____

_____

_____

_____

_____

_____

_____
_____
_____
_____
_____
_____
_____
_____
_____
_____
_____

My Purpose

_____
_____
_____
_____

My Calling

_____
_____
_____
_____

Week Eleven: Making it Happen!

Day Seven   *Date:*

Our life is focused forward,
but we seek to understand it by reflecting backward

Day of Reflection

Taking time to reflect will help you learn from your wins and losses. They both provide important lessons when applied, you can grow wiser and therefore be more effective in fulfilling your purpose. You have been discovering your passion, your life's purpose and calling these past few days. It is important to make sure you have this concept pinned down. It is a solid foundation to what you are about to discover. Now that you have identified your calling, you are ready discover the second of the two main ingredients in your growth, your *calling* and your *why*.

If you want to rise to a higher level, don't ever lose sight of your purpose. You also need to have a clear view of your calling and your why. Without them your life will be a vessel with no sail, stuck in the middle of the ocean unable to move. You may have wind, but you will be unable to capitalize on it. The vessel will drift without direction, and most likely end up capsizing in the first storm. Everything else would be a blur without having a clear understanding of your calling and your why.

Embark in this journey, establish your *calling,* and discover your *why*; which are two of the most vital forces impulsing you to living a life of fulfillment. Live, learn, love your life and if you don't, know you have the power to change it.

Things to Ponder:

1. What new revelation you have learned this week?
2. Name one thing within your gifts and talents you have started working on improving.
3. What steps have you taken so far or plan to take soon, as part of you plan.

Notes:

_____

_____

_____

_____

_____

_____

_____

_____

_____

_____

_____

_____

_____

_____

_____

_____

_____

_____

_____

_____

_____

_____

_____

_____

_____

_____

_____

_____

Week Twelve: Life Powers

Day One   *Date:*

Day One   *Date:*

Learn from the past, plan for the future,

and live in the present.

The Power of Time

There are 4 important powers in our lives:

1)   The power of Time
2)   The power of our Mindset
3)   The power of Words
4)   The power of my "Why".

Let's start today by addressing the power of "Time":

You either live in the past, the present or the future. It is vital to understand the power *"time"* has in our lives. Living in the *NOW* time zone is living in the present time. It is the time to enjoy and create memories today. Dwelling in your past will lead to a very toxic life full of guilt and regret. Just as bad, is living in the uncertainty of the future being worn down by stress and anxiety. You should only look back to reflect and learn, and forward to plan and set goals, but you must not dwell in your past and previous decisions nor worry about what the future will bring.

The book of Romans 8:29 SHBV states, "We know that all things work together for good to those that love God, who are called according to His purpose." There is no use worrying about the future, or the past. You can't resolve it any way… My father use to say, "Worry is a waste; if it has a solution, why worry? And if it doesn't, why worry anyway?" Life must go on. When we live a purpose fulfilling life, at the end, all things work for the best. If you pay attention, you will always find a life's message in every misfortune.

In life is not so much about the issue of our mistakes, it is about NOT dwelling on them. You must learn from them and move on or else you will be stuck in a place of regret and discontent. Regret is an unproductive state of mind. Dwelling on that state of regret will get you stuck on the past, unproductive, keeping you from moving forward.

On the other hand, when you live in the future, you live with anxiety. You develop the fear of the unknown. Don't get me wrong, it's good to envision, and plan. What you can't afford to do is dwelling in a place of uncertainty entangled by worry. Consider how important it is to know where you invest your energy. You either spend your energy regretting the past, dealing with anxiety, and the uncertainty tomorrow will bring, or you live in the present time focused on producing good things and creating memories today for tomorrow. The NOW moment is the reality of your life. It's the only time worth living. Take advantage of every moment life gives you, now, to enjoy and cherish.

Meditate on this thought; you receive a daily gift of 24 hours in which you devote 8 hours to sleep, 8 hours to work and 8 hours to enjoy. How you decide to spend or invest this gift, how you will spend the 8 productive and 8 leisure hours is your option. Quality of time is essential. Time is your most valuable asset, and there is no sense in wasting it. You must make the most of the time you have, every second spent will never be recovered. Decide today if you want to be productive with your time and use it wisely to fulfill your calling. Get to work and reach your goals instead of wasting your resources (time). Time is a present! Your *present* is a *present* (gift) you receive every day. What you do with it is your decision. Remember to be grateful for the daily portion of time you get. Never waste the opportunity time offers. Its yours! Are you ready to put it to productive use? Or will you let it run like water through your fingers? There is nothing more valuable than time, you can't save it, there is no putting it away for later. It's your most valuable asset, don't waste it!

Things to ponder:

1. In what tense do you live in? Past (regret), present (action), or future (anxious)?
2. Are you taking advantage of your time? Do you block time every day for the to-dos, or do you tend to procrastinate and waste time?

3. Can you commit to implementing better time management to do what you say you will do for the sake of progress?

Notes:

_____

_____

_____

_____

_____

_____

_____

_____

_____

_____

_____

_____

_____

_____

_____

_____

_____

_____

_____

_____

_____

_____

_____

_____

_____

Week Twelve: My Life Powers

Day Two   Date:

If you change your mindset, you can change the outcome.

The Power of the Mindset

Mindset exercises are an incredibly strong power in your life. Everything stems from your thoughts. Your mindset directly influences who you are, how you feel, and the outcome of your lives. We have the power to create with what we think and how we think. Your thought process and belief system can create, both positive and negative self-perpetuating cycles. Therefore, you can strip a millionaire of all their money, and given the chance, they will make it all over again. How? That is right, it's in their mindset, their mentality, the way they process information. What you think of yourself will eventually turn into your reality. Your self-perception can limit us or push us to limitless potential.

Your emotions are affected by your thoughts, what you speak is the result of your thoughts. If you feed your thoughts of anger, bitterness, and vengeance then your speech will reflect those thoughts, which will ultimately trigger your actions. If you think of yourself as a failure, you will feed yourself with doubt and end up feeling like a failure. Thus, you will become a failure. You will unconsciously adopt failure driven behavior. You must cast out all negative thoughts in your mind because they will drive you to negative results. Be conscious of the way you think about your plans, about yourself and about others. Your thoughts may turn into self-fulfilling prophecies dictating what your life will look like down the line in the future.

Ultimately, your mindset will determine outcome. The purpose of this journal is to transform your mindset and as a result change the outcome of your plans and life. It will ultimately take you in a path of successes. Be cautious of your thoughts! As you think, you shall become!

Things to ponder:

1. What kind of thoughts do you feed your mind? Positive and hopeful, or Negative and fearful?

2. Are you aware of your trend of thought? Can you identify a pattern of thought that leads your life?

Make sure to practice awareness, be aware of your thought pattern.

Notes:

_____

_____

_____

_____

_____

_____

_____

_____

_____

_____

_____

_____

_____

_____

_____

_____

_____

_____

_____

_____

_____

Week Twelve: My Life Powers

Day Three   *Date:*

And God said, "Let there be light," and there was light.

-Genesis 1:3 NKJV

The Power of Words

The power of the spoken word is the power to create. Evidence of it is that the world was created by the spoken word of God. God said let it be light, and there was light. He created the world through a variety of commands. We are created in His image, and therefore, we have the same creative power. We can speak positively to create and nourish, or we can speak negatively to destroy and tear down. We must be careful in choosing the right words to speak. We must speak to create and edify, not to kill or destroy. We can speak life, or we can speak death to our bodies, to our finances, our business, opportunities, and to people around us.

Through negative words you can create vicious circles turning into curses by creating repeated negative behaviors generating a polarizing destructive environment. Who we associate with, and the environment we move around directly influences the outcome of our lives. We must emphasize speaking with optimism to create encouraging moments influencing our environment with positive results.

You can choose to speak words of hope and faith to create an upbeat environment where you can flourish or you can choose judgment, which will trigger resentment, break-ups, and destruction. When we speak, we do so out of the abundance of our heart. Our heart is a fountain that outpours intensions expressed in words. Be very cautious of your choice of words. Don't be harsh in judgment, to yourself and others. Be vigilant not to curse your work by speaking negatively about your plans and goals, or making negative declarations over your life, finances, and the environment you live in. Instead speak well-being, goodness, speak hope, prosperity to your plans, your goals, and all your endeavors. The more positive you speak the more prosperous you will become. Have you ever "called" a chair, or a spot in the car or the table with friends or siblings? Think of it as you are "calling" the things you declare for yourself, good and/or bad.

Let's be clear! The power of the spoken words must be accompanied by the proper actions. Things will not happen by just mere declaration. You must put yourself in action by taking the proper steps to make things happen. Wishing and declaring alone will not make it happen, but it sure is a basic ingredient of prosperity. Let me be clear about this, the words we declare will create the right environment instilling growth because of your actions. Don't expect any results if no action is taken. C'mon, flip the switch to a better you!

Exercise: Listen to you speaking, be aware of the way you speak to yourself and others. How would you describe your speech mode, attitude, and your choice of words?

Questionnaire:

Do you often use foul language?	Y/N
Do you speak down to/about your plans?	Y/N
Do you gossip?	Y/N
During get-togethers with friends?	Y/N
Does cursing affects your mood?	Y/N
Does it trigger negative emotions?	Y/N
Do you speak to yourself in a negative way?	Y/N
Are you hard, unmerciful on yourself?	Y/N

Things to ponder:

1. Do you sabotage success thinking you're not capable or not worthy of good things? Are always expecting something bad to happen?
2. Do you feed on positive or negative thoughts?
3. When you have negative thoughts, do you recognize, acknowledge, and correct them? Or do you feed your mind with them?
4. How are your thoughts affecting daily performance?

Think of ways you can adjust and change the language you use to uplift your days and and/or your life, honor God, our creator, according to your beliefs, with the way you speak and how you express yourself. Apply self-awareness to change any negative speech for positive speech and make a record of how changing the choice of words has transformed outcome.

Notes:

_____

_____

_____

_____

_____

_____

_____

_____

_____

_____

_____

_____

_____

_____

_____

_____

_____

_____

_____

_____

_____

_____

Week Twelve: My Life Powers

Day Four   *Date*

There are 18 inches from the mind to the heart.

The Power of Your "WHY"

Your "why" is the foundation of the calling for your life, yet so many people live with no sense of direction unable to fulfill their purpose. Thus, your "Why" is the source of your motivation.

I have learned through the years that the answer to your "WHY" is not superficial, it lies deep in the roots of your heart. To find it, you need to dig deep, very deep to discover what really ignites the fire of motivation within you. You need to unveil what really gives you the desire to keep going, conquer fear, move forward, and fight for your goals. Thus, identifying your why is critical in reaching success. It is a key ingredient to keep you motivated.

Success is not about luck; it is about creating a pattern of habits helping you to move up the ladder. You need to start by identifying your true passion and your calling, which you should have already done last week. If you have not done so, go back and revisit last week's lessons. It is fundamentally important. Your why, on the other hand, is uprooted by asking questions, until the real why is identified. Your "Why" needs to be anchored to avoid drifting away and ultimately getting lost in the vast ocean of possibilities with no destination in sight. Very many people abandon ship, too many people give up just before breakthrough, and countless people never reach their utmost potential for their lack of direction.

When things don't go your way, when things seem like they are just not moving forward no matter how much you try, when relationships seem like they are just deteriorating and nothing seems to get through….at that point of breakdown, what pushes you to keep moving forward? What keeps you from giving up? Is it your goals, your needs, your most inner desires, or your relentless personality?

A crisis will reveal two main things, your true self and your WHY! Don't be satisfied with a shallow answer. Be shovel ready to keep digging deep in your heart to discover your WHY. It will be the anchor keeping you from drifting out to sea.

It's time to start digging!

I learned this strategy from a webpage I stumbled across by mere accident, it is www.7levelsdeep.com. Feel free to visit the website and do the exercise to discover your why. If you do, make sure to transpose your answers to the journal. The strategy is for you to ask yourself, "why is it important for me to succeed?" For every answer you give yourself, ask yourself why again and again digging seven levels deep. You ask until your real "why" is unveiled.

Seven is the number of perfection and completeness, and your "WHY" lies seven levels deep in your heart. The "why" questions will depend on your answers so keep asking yourself the why question until your true why is uprooted. Please beware that, as you dig deep you may find it painful, it may hurt, but it will be very rewarding for you at the end. I assure you that you will never be the same after you finish this exercise. Once identified, you need to continuously read your why to never lose sight of it. I suggest that once your final "WHY" is revealed, you post it by your desk, on your screen saver or somewhere conspicuous you can't miss to see it every day of your life!

Things to ponder:

1. What gets you out of bed every morning?
2. What motivates you to keep on going?
3. What is your WHY?
Keep your "Why" handy, cherish it, and review it every so often as you reach goals. Use it to remind yourself of what keeps you going!

Set it on your computer screen, or on a sticker posted next to your computer, …. Frame it or maybe paste it on your bathroom mirror to look at every morning. Whatever works for you…. just make it happen!

I. Why is it important for me to succeed?

_____

_____

_____

_____

_____

II. WHY?

_____

_____

_____

_____

_____

III. WHY?

_____

_____

_____

_____

_____

IV. WHY?

_____

_____

_____

_____

_____

V. WHY?

_____
_____
_____
_____
_____

VI. WHY?

_____
_____
_____
_____
_____

VII. WHY?

_____
_____
_____
_____

My Why is:

_____
_____
_____
_____
_____

Week Twelve: My Life Powers

Day Five   Date:

Faith without works is dead -James 2:20 HSBV

Your Action Plan

Let me make something crystal clear, spoken words create the environment for which things are created. Apart from what you may believe in, this is about the spiritual realm of things, a higher leveled dimension. To bring the spiritual realm into the natural realm we live in, we must take action to make this transition possible. Let me put this into perspective. Things start with a thought, a vision, and a goal, then you create the environment by which they will materialize. Once in the right environment you will "take action", so they can materialize and finally come to life. Its manifestation is through steps and actions taken to accomplish what is needed to bring things to life, from the spiritual into the natural realm. You must also need to be in the proper mental state. This is the reason you need to make certain mindset changes to reach a state of mind that is proper for these transitions to occur.

Think about a piece of land a farmer has chosen for farming and is getting ready to plant seeds. Do you just throw the seeds, or do you prepare the soil? The answer is, you prepare the soil for seeds to germinate and grow. If you keep putting these necessary actions off, then procrastination will sabotage your chances. You need to commit to stop procrastinating. You need to transition from a goal setter to an action taker. Once a goal is set, you are ready to get to work. *Faith is the currency of the spiritual, action is the currency of the natural.*

With this in mind, outline actionable assignments based on a timeline you will set for yourself. An efficient action plan will outline all the steps required to achieve your goal(s) to reach your target with efficacy by the assigned timeline. You need an expected start date and end date not only for the entire project, but for every step and task required in the process.

Once your goals are set, following these steps may help you get your call to action started:

Action Plan:

Step 1:
    What: Actions (Required steps to achieve your goals)
    Who: Person/Team (Who oversees each step)
    When: Timeline (Deadline for each step)
Step 2:
    Identify Resources (What do you need for each step?)
    Identify Barriers (What can potentially hinder your progress)
    Identify Outcomes (Desired result for each step)
Step 3: Follow up and follow through to completion.

Things to Ponder:

1. Are you willing to commit to "take action" and make things happen?
     Yes, or no?
2. You can start by designing a plan of action as outlined above, for every one thing you want to accomplish in your life. Do you want to start a business? or maybe a project? Lose weight? Get better grades?
3. The goal does not matter, if you follow the steps, you will reach them.

Now that you have reviewed all 4 Life Powers …

answer the following:

My Weak Power _____

My Strong Power: _____

Notes:

Week Twelve: My Life Powers

Your Commitment

The end of the journal is the beginning of your transformation. You have learned many lessons throughout this 12-week journey. These lessons must be *implemented, applied, and practiced*, otherwise this will be just another book on the shelf. The decision is yours. How you apply what you have learned will determine how far you will go with these transformational changes you decided to implement. It is completely your decision, your desire, your call, your responsibility. This is solely on you. You own it! Now that you know your passion, your why, and your purpose you are ready to set goals, build an action plan, and follow through to accomplishment.

Now you should have a better sense of direction than you did when you first started the journal, and where you will be headed from this point forward. Remember to start with accomplishing one task early in your day. The easiest task is making your bed and keeping your room and closet organized, it will save you time every morning. This one task will set you off to a good start every day. Once you accomplish your first task of the day, you are ready to accomplish many more!

I suggest you go back to revisit the journal in another three, six months and at the end of the year. Reviewing it every so often, take notes, and write down the seven main things you want to change in your life. There is always room for improvement. This is a lifetime commitment, it's a way of life. Fill in the list below and sign it to seal the deal. Hereon, make sure to apply what you've learned throughout this journal. Write down the 3 steps on page 203 in the Call-to-Action plan for every change outlined below. Remember step #3, follow up and follow through until the goal is accomplished. Never give up!

Change #1:

_____

_____

_____

Start Date: _____

Target Date: _____

Accomplished Date: _____

Action:_____

_____

_____

_____

_____

Goal:_____

_____

_____

Change #2:

_____

_____

_____

Start Date: _____

Target Date: _____

Accomplished Date: _____

Action:_____

_____

_____

_____

_____

Goal:_____

_____

_____

_____

_____

Change #3:

_____

_____

_____

Start Date: _____

Target Date: _____

Accomplished Date: _____

Action:_____

_____

_____

_____

_____

Goal:

_____   _____

_____

_____

_____

_____

Implementation is the last phase of accomplishments, don't ever underestimate its power. A commitment is an empty promise until its implemented!

MY COMITMENT

I hereby acknowledge and commit to implementing the above transformational changes in the next 12 months and to take the steps necessary to bring about these changes in my life. I am aware it is solely my responsibility to follow through until changes are accomplished.

Print Your Name: _____

_____
Signature
Signed on: ____/____/_____

Week Twelve: My Life Powers

Day Seven   *Date*

Your **Words** Become your **Actions**,

Your **Actions** Become your **Habits**,

Your **Habits** Become your **Values**,

Your **Values** Become your **Destiny**!

Day of Reflection:

Your Values, Your Choice!

- *The value of TIME*: Time is our most valuable asset; and we tend to waste it when we think we have a lot of it. The truth is, we really have no way to know how much time we have left. Every second you waste you will never recover. You can't save it for later, so make the best of every second and every minute you are given. Make it your #1 investment.

- *The value of TODAY*: We spend our youth wanting to be older, to do other things only older people do, wasting the opportunity to enjoy early years; then when we grow old, we desire to be young again and live searching for the fountain of youth. Don't live as if you would never die, to then die like you never lived. Appreciate the gift today offers!

- *The value of HEALTH*: Don't waste your health trying make money. Focus on yourself while you are at it because then you will waste your money trying to recover your health. Be a good steward of your body, take care of your health as part of your journey!

- *The value of LOVE*: Love is the most valuable gift someone can give you; it is a decision you make to give it and who you give it to. You can't buy love; you can't force love. It is a voluntary gift given and expressed in the smallest of gestures, a smile, a helping hand, a word of encouragement, to name a few. However, for some people it is difficult to give love and receive love, for one it is perceived as weakness in our culture. Break that paradigm and make a difference. Decide to spread love seeds and enjoy the harvest!

- *The value in HAVING*: We come into this world with nothing, and we leave with nothing. The real value is not in what we have, but who we have, and who we can count on. The material things rot, the inner spirit lives. Nurture the spiritual you, and if you are blessed with abundance share it. There is more growth and fulfilment in giving than in receiving. Give and grow abundantly!

- *The value of MONEY*: Wealth is not found on that who has the most, it is who needs less. It lies on the freedom prosperity provides.

- *The value in PEOPLE*: Your physique attracts, but your personality, your values, your inner being makes one fall in love and find true love.

- *The value of GRATEFULNESS*: Be grateful of what you have. Those who do not value what they have, some day will lament losing it. Appreciate the fact that you have been blessed with all you have, good health, your family, your friends, your job, your car, your home, etc. Count your blessings!

- *The Value in the good SEED*: What you sow, is what you reap. The seeds represent your actions, and the harvest, the fruit of what you sow. Beware of the seeds you are spreading. If you don't like the harvest, change the seeds.

- *The value in FREEDOM*: Living free of grief, pain, regrets, bitterness, victim mentality, addictions, dependency….is evidence of a healing heart. We hurt through life, and that we can't control. What we can control, is how we process offenses. Keep your heart free, don't allow wounds to take over your life! Forgive, heal and be free…

- *The value in FORGIVENESS*: Forgiving is letting go. The more you hold on to grudges, the more your heart will grow bitter. Remember, you speak from the heart. The heart is the fountain of emotions. Whatever you speak flows from your heart. The heart is your treasure box, guard it!

I leave you this to ponder:

We go through life facing challenges, confronted by tough choices, and making decisions throughout the day, every day. It's expected, and you will inevitably make mistakes along the way. *Be humble to admit your mistakes, courageous enough to confront them, and wise enough to correct them.* Be intentional and embrace change. Today aim higher than you reached yesterday and always do more than required. Intentionally go the extra mile! Embrace daily challenges, they are your daily vitamin dose to spur your growth. Never cease to seek for more. Always seek to grow, because if you stop, and when you do, your life… is officially over!

You can share your testimony by sending an email to:
Mystory@laurinaemiliani.com

Works Cited

Brainyquote. (2022). *BrainyQuote*. Retrieved from
    https://www.brainyquote.com/authors

Dispenza, D. J. (2019). *Becoming Spernatural*. Carlsbad, California: Hay
    House, Inc.

Garcia, J. &. (2017). *Hay Esperanza*. Miami, Florida: Editorial Hay
    Esperanza.

Klein, P. (n.d.). *7 Levels Deep*. Retrieved from 7Discover your Why:
    http://www.7levelsdeep.com

Meyer, J. (2022). *Joyce Meyer Ministries*. Retrieved from JoyceMeyer.org:
    https://joycemeyer.org/everydayanswers/ea-teachings/a-brand-new-
    say

Salomon. (2009). *The Book of Proverbs*. Holman Christian Standard Bible.

University of West Alabama. (2019, May 17). Retrieved from UWA.com:
    https://online.uwa.edu/infographics/basic-emotions/

Maxwell, John C. (2012). *The 15 Invaluable Laws of Growth*.
    New York, NY USA The Hachette Book Group 2014.

Made in the USA
Las Vegas, NV
07 September 2023

77209855R00125